3   COMBINE CITY A
    To give meaning t
    bring about uniqu
    urban and natural
    interconnectedne

4   ANTICIPATE CHA
    To honour the evolution of the city we will incorporate
    generous flexibility and adaptability in our plans
    and programs, in order to facilitate unpredictable
    opportunities for future generations.

5   CONTINUE INNOVATION
    To advance the city we will encourage improved
    processes, technologies and infrastructures, and we
    will support experimentation and the exchange of
    knowledge.

6   DESIGN HEALTHY SYSTEMS
    To sustain the city we will utilize 'cradle to cradle'
    solutions, recognizing the interdependence, at all
    scales, of ecological, social and economic health.

7   EMPOWER PEOPLE TO MAKE THE CITY
    Acknowledging citizens to be the driving force in
    creating, keeping and sustaining the city, we facilitate
    opportunities for our citizens to pursue their unique
    potential, with spirit and dignity.

The words of the Almere Principles will come alive
and become meaningful through human action,
by incorporating them on each level into every design
for the city as whole.

The Almere Principles

For an ecologically, socially and economically sustainable future of Almere 2030

THOTH PUBLISHERS BUSSUM

The Almere Principles and the explanation included in
this book were drawn up under the responsibility of the
Municipal Executive of the Municipality of Almere with the
unanimous support of the Municipal Council.
The text of the Almere Principles and the corresponding
explanation were written in collaboration with the
Municipality of Almere and the firm of William McDonough
+ Partners.
With special thanks to Joost Schrijnen, Alex van Oost,
Diane Dale and Michelle Amt.

© 2008 The authors, the Municipality of Almere,
Postbus 200, NL-1300 AE Almere
and THOTH Publishers, Nieuwe 's-Gravelandseweg 3
NL-1405 HH Bussum
WWW.THOTH.NL

Editor: Fred Feddes
Text contributions: Jacqueline Cramer, Adri Duivesteijn,
William McDonough, Fred Feddes
Translations: WTS Vertalingen B.V., Bunnik
Images: Municipality of Almere, Atelier Structuurvisie
2030+; except for p. 43: Nederlands Architectuurinstituut,
Rotterdam / Van Eesteren-Fluck Collection and
Van Lohuizenstichting, The Hague
Production: Yolanda Musson and Fred Feddes
Graphic design: Bart de Haas, The Hague
Printing: drukkerij Mart.Spruijt bv, Amsterdam
Binding: Boekbinderij van Waarden, Zaandam

FSC APPROVED PAPER
This book was printed on 100-gram Freelife Vellum paper bearing the
FSC quality mark. The Forest Stewardship Council (FSC) quality mark
stands for the promotion of the responsible production of wood, with
respect to both the environmental aspects of wood production as well
as the social aspects. Currently, 13 percent of the wood used in the
Netherlands is FSC certified.

All rights reserved. No part of this publication may be reproduced or
transmitted in any form or by any means, electronic or mechanical,
including photocopying, recording, or any form or by any means,
electronic or mechanical, including photocopying, recording, or
any information storage and retrieval system, without permission in
writing from the publisher.

ISBN 978 90 6868 484 1

Contents

6   Foreword
    JACQUELINE CRAMER

8   The Almere Principles: a manifesto for sustainable development
    ADRI DUIVESTEIJN

19   Sustaining Design for a Cradle to Cradle Future
    WILLIAM MCDONOUGH

24   The Almere Principles explained

42   In the old Almere style
    In search of Almere principles *avant la lettre*
    FRED FEDDES

73   The first exercise for the Principles in Almere
    An impression of the introduction in April 2008
    FRED FEDDES

Foreword

By 2030, Almere will be the fifth largest city in the Netherlands. It will be a green city where 350,000 people will live and work happily in a healthy environment. It will adopt various styles and atmospheres, from metropolitan and compact to green and countrified. There, you will travel to work by bike, and you can also get there comfortably by car or train. Almere City is in touch with the water. It enriches the natural environment of the IJmeer and respects the green landscape beyond the area towards Utrecht. Almere is part of the North Wing of the urbanized area known as Randstad, where major construction programmes are planned between now and 2030. Quantity is not the only aspect considered in agreements reached between national government and the municipalities and provinces concerned. All parties must also devote themselves to the quality of the built and unbuilt environment. These qualities include oneness with the surroundings, accessibility, sustainability, climate change proof, and the relationship between residential living and the green-and-blue environment. The growth of Almere plays a major role in this. We have to start today with decisions on how to meet this challenge. We have to draw the contours within which the increase in scale or 'Scale Jump' and the doubling of the city will take shape. It is important to have the conditions for an attractive, green and sustainable city created at this very first stage. I am pleased that the municipality of Almere is setting the tone with the 'Almere Principles'. This will provide a boost to practical sustainability, especially because the municipality has involved William McDonough – co-founder of the *Cradle-to-Cradle* approach to the economy of recycling and sustainable chain management – in the drafting of the Principles. I myself was present at the unveiling of the Almere Principles. They contain beautiful, powerful words. Now, it will all come down to putting these principles into practice by applying cradle-to-cradle methods concretely at all levels (regional, city, district, building) and to the multiform relationship between land and water. The Almere Principles will serve as the reference standard for all concrete elaborations.

I support Almere's aspirations wholeheartedly. As none of us knows what a sustainable scale jump of this magnitude looks like in practice – Almere is unique! – Almere deserves an opportunity to experiment.

I congratulate Almere on its Almere Principles. Not commandments, but an effective set of benchmarks to fall back on. This is how support and enthusiasm are created for the highly sustainable aspirations cherished by the municipality. Becoming the fifth largest city in the Netherlands is no easy task. This will prove even more difficult to do, with a view towards fitting the city in with its environment and the quality, climate, sustainability, along with a balanced relationship with the water. There lies the new horizon. Good luck, Almere!

JACQUELINE CRAMER
Minister of Housing, Spatial Planning and the Environment

The Almere Principles: a manifesto for sustainable development

ADRI DUIVESTEIJN

Almere's second beginning
"Civilizations of the past have regarded cities as neither shameful nor inevitable, but as deliberate creations, worth making sacrifices to build, maintain, and embellish", according to the historian Donald Olsen in his book *The city as a work of art*.
It is an inspirational pronouncement that not only applies to the 'civilisations of the past', but which may likewise apply to our own time and to our own civilisation. This credo applies all the more accurately to Almere, a city which, in a span of forty years, came into being as a deliberate creation, and which has remained in the making to this day. We are therefore more than justified in our strong efforts involved in the 'building, maintenance and embellishment' of the existing and future city. The Almere Municipal Executive, of which I am a member, is fully aware of this cultural task. The Executive has put the 'Almere Principles' into the perspective of this task, and has acquired backing for these from the full Municipal Council.
The pronouncement by Olsen is particularly apt, now that Almere is preparing for a new beginning in the city's history. Together with the region and the State, Almere has set an enormous task for itself for the years leading up to 2030. In order to relieve the burden in the northern part of the Randstad, another 60,000 homes will be built in Almere between the years 2010 and 2030. Almere must also add another 100,000 jobs. As a result of this 'Schaalsprong Almere' [literally, a 'leap in scale' or 'Scale Jump'], the population and the built-up area will double between now and the year 2030.

Yet it is not the quantitative specifications which are the most important. With the aid of the Scale Jump, "the city will develop its own recognisable identity with full economic and social facilities", the government wrote in the *Noordvleugelbrief* [North Wing Paper] (2006), setting out the long-term agreements for this part of the Randstad. "The city is not only growing, but developing to become a complete, balanced city, with metropolitan facilities. It is not so much the building of a 'VINEX wijk' [new suburbs built in the 1990's as part of a national plan to increase the housing stock in the Netherlands], but the gradual ongoing development of a complete city with approximately 350,000 residents". The preparations are in full swing. The deadline for the completion of the *Structuurvisie Almere 2030+* [Almere Structural Vision for 2030 and beyond], which will clarify the nature and direction the Scale Jump will take, is late 2009.

The Scale Jump is a new assignment, which requires new answers to the needs and wants of today and tomorrow. Sustainability and ecology are the central themes, and the reasons for and specific details of this will be elaborated on below. However, before do this, we will consider how closely the Scale Jump is linked to the existing city, and to Almere's forty-year history of thinking, designing, building, experiencing and changing. In order to be well-prepared for the future, it is vital to first examine the original ideas, ideals and plans for Almere such as these evolved during the years 1961 to 1983. Almere's second beginning builds on this first beginning. As we look back on the past, we do this in order to be able to gain a clearer view of the future.

The topicality of the original design
What is still truly appealing about the early years of Almere is the earnestness and the idealism with which the 'godfathers of Almere' went about their task. They made a number of fundamental design choices which are still very much alive and future-oriented. The choices made back then still determine the city's character today, and they imply the promises of what is still possible in the future.

One crucial design choice from the early years is the relationship between the built-up area and the surrounding country, between 'red' and 'green'. It was decided that all of the residents of Almere had to be able to live close to the countryside. To achieve this, the 'red' was distributed across several cores, separated by as-yet unheard of generous expanses of greenery. This design aroused a great deal of criticism in professional circles at the time. The plan was considered 'anti-urban' and it would inevitably result in a 'suburbia' according to the American model. However, by emphasising what it was *not*, namely not urban, the critics overlooked what it in fact *was*, and what it could be. The Almere model seems to possess an impressive capacity to absorb, enabling it to truly grow to become a full-fledged city over time, arising from the vast green framework. This growth process has yet not come to an end. Almere has the character of a suburban city with a number of (highly) urban moments within – such as the new city centre, the Kemphaan, the Boathouse and the Kustzone Haven/Poort [Coastal Zone] – and thanks to the flexible design created back then, there is still plenty of room to grow.

A second vital choice involves the relationship between the individual cores and the city as a whole. The building of Almere did not concentrate on a single location, but was spread out across several cores or nuclei. This allowed each core to develop its own identity and history from the very beginning, and this individual identity will remain recognisable during the continued growth of the core or the city as a whole. This recognisability is a quality one would normally only find in older cities. With their polynuclear or multi-core design, the godfathers succeeded in introducing contrast, identity and history into a still young city. The significance of this only increases in strength as the city develops further. What started as a polynuclear city, is transforming into a city with multiple cores. Although each of the cores retains its own character and history, a new type of growth is gradually developing which transcends each of the individual cores. The unusual naming used in Almere illustrates this. The individual cores are called Almere Haven [Harbour], Almere Stad [City] and Almere Buiten

[Outside], and then Almere Poort, Almere Pampus and Almere Hout or Almere Oost. 'Almere' can continue to multiply, each time with a new nucleus, a new name, and with its own identity. And yet, they are all still Almere. With the creation of each new core, the whole gains a new dimension.
A third design choice determines the relationship between Almere and its surroundings. The structural plan for the Southern IJsselmeer polders, dating from 1961, makes it clear that the new polders fulfilled a key role in the improvement of the national road and rail infrastructure. The area which would later be the site for Almere was laid with excellent connections on all sides. Obviously, the design was heavily oriented toward the Randstad, but it also provided for excellent connections with the rest of the polders and the surrounding older land. The double road connection to Amsterdam was crucial: via Muiden and via the Markerwaard. However, the impoldering of the Markerwaard fell through, and the search for a way to compensate this 'amputation' of the original design for Almere's infrastructure has gone on for thirty years now.
These three design choices are now also part of the preparation for the Scale Jump. In actual fact, we are confronted with the same questions: how do we approach the relationship between 'red' and 'green' (and 'blue'), how do we approach the relationship between the individual (old and new) nuclei and the city as a whole, and how should we design the relationships between Almere and its surroundings? These questions were not only asked at the time, but were also answered. We can now fall back on these past answers, we can continue along the same lines, and we can give them a new meaning. The more we delve into the original plans for Almere, the more we realise that we do not really have to come up with so many new ideas. The outlines of the possible long-term development of Almere were already plotted out decades ago, and fortunately, we will be able to use these for the next thirty years.

Sustainability as a theme
In short, the Scale Jump is the next step in the tradition of Almere's growth. There is a high degree of continuity and

progress, and we can make the current plans for the future more comprehensive by keeping the plans from the past in mind. However, that is only half of the story. Continuity does not mean changelessness. The circumstances of today are very different from those forty years ago, and thus the plans for Almere's second beginning must satisfy requirements other than those set out in the plans for the first beginning. Sustainability is the main theme in which the municipality and the state summarise the demands the Scale Jump must fulfil. In the UpR contract 'Almere 2030+' which they concluded in 2007 as a follow-up to the *Noordvleugelbrief*, they have worded it as follows: "The state and Almere have the joint ambition of implementing the themes of sustainability and ecology as the primary, guiding principles in urban development." There are several reasons for this.

It would be impossible for anyone building a city today to ignore the major ecological and environmental issues involved in climate change, energy, raw materials and waste. The urban development of the twenty-first century must provide a solution to these problems. Not only in terms of ecology, but the social and economic welfare as well as stability are also involved. Anyone avoiding these themes – because they are too expensive, too complicated, too difficult – is acting without foresight. In a city located below sea level, it is inconceivable to fail to take the necessity of sustainability into consideration.

It is better and more profitable to face the challenge presented by sustainability issues from the very start, and to search for radically better solutions. If there are not yet any solutions, we must create these. If we invent these for Almere, then they might just come in handy elsewhere in the world. The choice for sustainable urban development is therefore the choice for a vanguard position. This approach fits within the Almere tradition of trailblazing and experimentation. It also fits within the efforts made by the national government. It is with good reason that the Ministry of VROM [Housing, Spatial Planning and the Environment], Almere's partner in the Scale Jump, is involved in spatial planning as well as the environment. Almere's Scale Jump is an exemplary opportunity to link these two sectors with one another on a serious scale.

Moreover, sustainability is fundamentally linked to the field of urban development. Cities are born of the pursuit to create permanent forms for human co-existence. This is not always successful, and the strong population growth and urbanisation occurring since the nineteenth century have placed great demands on our ability to create a stable living environment for everyone. Nevertheless, good urban planning remains optimistic regarding the options for healthy cities. Pitted against the spectre of monster cities which exhaust the earth's resources, a hopeful prospect for sustainable urban development which restores this disrupted balance is necessary. As the European organisation of town planners, the ECTP, states in its *New Charter of Athens* from 2003: "Spatial planning is vital for the delivery of sustainable development".

And the reverse applies as well: ideas on sustainable development are essential to spatial planning. In the past, the long-term perspective in thinking about urban development was often derived from the great ideologies, but these have lost their power to give direction. What remains is the ideology of the market, which, in turn, falls short in social terms, in preserving immaterial values such as cohesion and integration, and in its application to demographic and spatial developments for the very long term. And yet, in building the city, we need a vision which supersedes self-interest and the political differences of today, and which is even capable of thinking generations ahead. Sustainability can serve as the core for this long-term vision, if only for the fact that it compels us to think far in advance. For example, climate change is a development which spans dozens if not hundreds of years, and if we are to think about solutions, we must also apply this same timeframe.

Sustainability is a vast concept within this approach. Ecological sustainability is indispensable, but in addition, the city also needs social and economic sustainability. A city must be able to live with change, it must be resilient, it must be able to renew its existence over the course of years or even centuries. The goal of sustainability does not need to be a defensive one. A positive approach is possible, one which entails confidence in human ability. We can take on the environmental problems with which we are confronted, on the condition that we want to do so, that we develop the knowledge required, and that we are willing to expend the effort.

Collaboration with William McDonough
In order to work out this positive approach to sustainability, Almere approached the American architect William McDonough. Together with the German chemist Michael Braungart, he developed the sustainability philosophy *Cradle to Cradle*, which achieved prominence in the Netherlands thanks to the VPRO television programme, *Tegenlicht* (October 2006, November 2007). The cradle-to-cradle approach views sustainability as a design issue. The goal is not to limit the ecological damage resulting from human actions slightly, but to design production processes in such a way that no damage occurs at all, and to replace this potential damage with profit. The goal is to design industrial processes which do not place a burden on the environment but instead, enrich them, to make buildings which do not consume energy, but yield it, and to create districts or cities which absorb CO_2 instead of producing it. For Almere, the cradle-to-cradle approach was not the only interesting aspect of their work; the same applied to its forerunner, the *Hannover Principles*, which McDonough and Braungart wrote in 1992 as part of the preparations for the Expo 2000 world fair in Hannover. Since sustainability was to be the theme of the Expo, the organisers asked them to draw up a design guideline for the architects of the country pavilions. The Expo has long since passed, but the Hannover Principles continue to remain a source of inspiration, among other reasons due to their practical focus and simultaneous radical and uncompromising nature. For example: "Eliminate the concept of waste", and: "Rely on natural energy flows".
Between Summer 2007 and Spring 2008, the firm of William McDonough + Partners and the municipality of Almere collaborated intensively on the Almere Principles.

McDonough and his staff members, Diane Dale and Michelle Amt, travelled frequently to Almere, and a small Almere work group visited the firm's office in the United States in March of 2008 to participate in an intensive work session. For the Almere Principles, the vigorous optimism of the Almere 'godfathers' and that of the Hannover Principles provided an important source of inspiration, as did the specific requirements and circumstances of the Scale Jump. The Almere Principles are the result of a close partnership. It was surprising to realise how much they are in keeping with the history of Almere. The Principles are not a magic formula for sustainability which has been dropped onto Almere out of the sky. They come from within. They build on the qualities which the city originally had, and they revive dormant qualities which are capable of eliminating the weaknesses of present-day Almere.

The product of this collaboration is brief and to the point. The Almere Principles contain seven starting points which one could learn by heart, with a brief introduction and conclusion. They fit on a single sheet of paper, or on a T-shirt. They contain very few details. During the preparations, we asked ourselves if they should concentrate specifically on Almere, or whether they should be universal in their application. Gradually, this problem solved itself: they do both. Anyone who goes one step below the Principles will find themselves in the middle of the concrete, practical example of Almere. And by going one step beyond, the Principles refer to tasks which are at hand all over the world.

The Almere Principles as a public manifesto and as a prelude to action

One distinguishing feature of the Almere Principles is their public nature. Drawing up a list of starting points for urban development is nothing new. Elsewhere in this book, you will find six 'objectives for Almere' dating back to 1974. They are well-formulated, have involved a great deal of thought, and they are surprisingly current. The major difference between these principles and the current Almere Principles is, they were hidden away in a report. The well-chosen wording of the 1974 document hardly plays a role in public debate.

We wanted to do it differently this time. For the Municipal Executive, it is obvious that a political and social debate should not only involve practicalities and details, but also the main issues, the principles and motives. An effective tool for this are manifestos and manifestations which, with their cultural slant and thought-provoking vistas, provide an incentive to rise above daily practice. This is also extremely important now. If we are going to double the size of Almere in the coming decades, we must constantly keep those great words in mind which guide our actions.

The future of Almere concerns everyone. It goes without saying that everyone should be able to actively contribute to building the new city. And so, it should also be self-evident to discuss the outlines of the principles before a public audience. Not only in the beginning, but constantly, every step of the way. The Almere Principles represent a public manifesto, that openly expresses the values that we find important for the city of tomorrow. They embed continuity in a way that can be readily identified and discussed by everyone. Creating a city means the building of a society, and a society cannot survive without communication, the exchange of knowledge and discussion. The Almere Principles are part of this discussion, at every level, now and in the decades to come. They must be made completely accessible to the public, as it should be in a city.

And these words must likewise be turned into actions. The Almere Principles must continue to do their job in the thoughts, plans and actions of all those people who are involved with Almere within the municipality's own organisation and beyond. That is not only the wish of the Executive, but also the message of the full Municipal Council of Almere, which collectively backed the motion of 28 June 2008 in respect of the Almere Principles. The Council "declares that the Almere Principles will be used as the guiding principles for the development of the entire city, including policymaking choices on the structural vision and the Integral Framework Agreement for Almere 2030+", and "requests that the Executive draw up a plan of action to flesh out the Almere Principles". It represents unambiguous support in the pursuit of sustainability. The unanimity of

the Council increases the likelihood that the Almere Principles will remain overriding and inspiring over a longer period.
The plan of action demanded by the Council will be worked out in 2008. One crucial element in this is the new *DuurzaamheidsLab Almere* [Almere Sustainability Lab] which will function as the 'brain' of Almere's sustainability objective. The Sustainability Lab will gather knowledge and insights, build up a memory, create a network of government, experts, businesses and citizens, it will stimulate new ideas, will bring together a variety of disciplines and views, and it will link theory to practice. It will be involved with aspects of ecological sustainability (recycling, bio-diversity), social sustainability (emancipation, upward mobility, cohesion) and economic sustainability (sustainability as a selling point, the Sustainable Zonal Development Business & Science Center), and continue to be inspired by the major themes in the cradle-to-cradle approach, explained elsewhere in this publication by William McDonough. In addition to the Sustainability Lab, the municipality will apply the Almere Principles as the basis in evaluating its own Structural Vision, and as a standard measure in the sub-studies into the A6 zone, the Flevospoorzone, the Kustzone and Almere Hout. And whenever the municipality asks others to draft spatial plans, such as those for Almere Hout Noord, we invite them to internalise the Almere Principles in doing so.
One thing that must be prevented is for the Almere Principles to become fixed into a package of rules or evaporate into marketing slogans. A government often has the tendency to translate the inspired words of a declaration of principles into rules and quantifiable standards; a market party has the similar inclination to hide mediocre acts behind persuasive words. In both cases, the significance that the Almere Principles could hold for the future of the city are undermined. The true challenge is to prevent this.
The Almere Principles do not offer certainty, they are not a recipe that we can follow blindly, they are not intended as hype or a gimmick. On behalf of the Executive, I would like to invite you to use the Almere Principles as a conscientious

frame of reference in the dialogue on the future, and as a source of inspiration for self-reflection. The discussion about the future of Almere is in full swing. Since they were presented to the Municipal Council, to a large group of experts and to stakeholders on 8 and 9 April 2008, the Almere Principles have been contributing to this debate. The discussions then and in the months that have followed have shown the Executive that the Almere Principles have a right to exist as a manifesto for sustainability. We hope that this effect is lasting and that the Almere Principles will continue to encourage us to give serious and fundamental thought to our own work, our credibility, and the consequences of our work for future generations. With the promise of a more sustainable and healthier Almere in 2030.

Adri Duivesteijn is alderman for spatial planning at the municipality of Almere

Sustaining Design for a Cradle to Cradle Future

WILLIAM MCDONOUGH

In 2007, William McDonough + Partners was asked by Gemeente Almere to help draft guiding principles for the development of their pioneering, thirty year old city as it doubles its population over the next thirty years; my colleagues and I were honoured to participate in such a unique and historic event. The fruits of this labour, *The Almere Principles*, embrace and build on the commitment to sustainability originally set forth in *The Hannover Principles*, the design guidelines my colleague, Michael Braungart, and I crafted for the city of Hannover 1993. *The Almere Principles* are envisaged as the next generation of *Hannover*, one that applies the original principles of sustainability to the specific task of developing the living city. They offer an inspiring and encompassing approach to urban design, one that is based on a regenerative, hopeful strategy for the future.

Almere is encountering the challenges facing many communities today. Can we grow in ways that do not compromise our existing quality of life and that protect and strengthen our identity? Can we use new development as an opportunity to address our economic, social and environmental problems? Can we make our community more livable? What do we want to grow into? While many of today's urban strategies create more livable cities – pedestrian-friendly neighbourhoods, more vital street life, plentiful green space – they ultimately fall short of a truly sustaining urbanism, one that addresses global challenges at the local level. Energy and transportation systems still burn fossil fuels; building materials sometimes harmful to human and environmental health continue to be used; precious water daily runs off impenetrable surfaces; urban manufacturing remains wasteful and unsafe; and economic activity is still not considered part of the designer's domain.

Most responses to these challenges seek to limit the impact of human activity by minimizing pollution and waste. However, there is another way. We often say that design is the first signal of intention, which raises the question – what are our intentions? Do we intend to create things that have only positive effects, or just fewer negative ones? Imagine buildings, neighbourhoods, transportation systems, factories and parks all designed to enhance a city's economic, environmental, and social health. Imagine urban designs that reach beyond sustainability to enrich lives.

To realize this vision, we can base our communities on the operating principles of the natural world. In essence, natural systems thrive on the free energy of the sun, which interacts with the geochemistry of the earth's surface to sustain productive and regenerative biological systems. Human systems designed to operate by these same laws can approach the effectiveness of the earth's diverse living systems, in which growth is inherently good and there is no such thing as waste.

These laws can be distilled into three key principles that allow designers to apply the intelligence of natural systems to human designs, and form the foundation of cradle to cradle thinking:

Waste equals food

In nature, the processes of every organism contribute to the health of the whole. One organism's waste becomes food for another and nutrients flow perpetually in regenerative, cradle to cradle cycles of birth, decay and rebirth. Design modelled on these virtuous cycles eliminates the very concept of waste. In the world of product design, for example, products and materials can be designed of components that return either to soil as a nutrient, or to industry for remanufacture at the same or higher level of quality. For cities like Almere, safe manufacturing and cradle to cradle material flows are crucial not only to ensure that the materials we build with will be healthy and beneficial, but also to provide a clean, productive economic base for healthy growth. By modelling our processes on nature, human industry can become a regenerative thread in the urban fabric.

Use current solar income
Nature's cradle to cradle cycles are powered by the energy of the sun. Trees and plants manufacture food from sunlight, an elegant, effective system that uses the earth's only perpetual source of energy income. The wind, a thermal flow fuelled by sunlight, can be tapped, and along with direct solar collection can generate enough power to meet the energy needs of entire cities and regions, and indeed, entire nations. Developing wind and solar power transforms our energy infrastructure, reconnects rural areas to cities through the cooperative exchange of energy and technology, and can one day end our reliance on fossil fuels. Clean energy, economic development, thousands of jobs – all by using the energy of the sun.

Celebrate diversity
Healthy ecosystems are complex communities of living things, each of which has developed a unique response to its surroundings that works in concert with other organisms to sustain the system. Each organism *fits* in its place and in each system the most *fitting* survive. Abundant diversity is the source of an ecosystem's strength and resilience. Urban designers can celebrate the diversity of regional landscapes and cultures, and grow ever more effective as they do so.

When these principles are applied to design of communities, astonishing things can happen. Safe, healthy materials maintained in biological or technical metabolisms create healthier residents, transform landfills into compost piles, and eliminate the need to mining the earth's crust for precious resources. Buildings designed to make the most of beneficial breezes and the warmth and light from the sun reconnect residents to the rhythms and delights of nature, in addition to providing excellent energy performance. Clean manufacturing revitalizes local economies and eliminates the need for regulation, bringing jobs and housing closer together and improving everyone's quality of life. A culture of innovation encourages start-up businesses and allows all residents the opportunity to determine their own future. Diverse public realms encourage openness, collaboration and connectivity through a range of spaces where residents meet, gather, socialize and engage with one another.

At its core, cradle to cradle design is a philosophy of hope. Imagine everything we make into a gesture that supports life, inspires delight, and expresses intelligence in harmony with nature. Imagine buildings like trees that harvest the energy of the sun, sequester carbon, make oxygen, distill water, provide habitat for thousands of species as well as generate more energy than they consume. Buildings with on-site wetlands and botanical gardens recovering nutrients from circulating water. Fresh air, flowering plants, and daylight everywhere. Birds nesting and feeding in a building's verdant footprint. Imagine, in short, buildings and communities as life-support systems in harmony with energy flows, human souls, and other living things.

With this vision in mind, we can imagine cities participating ever more creatively with nature; cities where skyscrapers harvest the energy of the sun, where rooftop gardens capture rain and become part of the watershed; where food and materials grown in the countryside, using implements and technology created in the city, are absorbed by the urban body and returned to their source as a form of waste that can replenish the system. Everything moves in regenerative cycles, from city to country, country to city, in natural and cultural networks that circulate biological nutrition – food, fiber, wood, water – and technical nutrition – the hardware and software of the twenty-first century. The metabolism of the living city encourages such flows of nutrients and thus allows human settlements and the natural world to flourish side by side

The end goal of cradle to cradle design is a delightfully diverse, safe, healthy and just world, with clean air, water, soil and power – economically, equitably, ecologically and elegantly enjoyed. As we work together toward this vision, we must be courageous; we are creating new ways of thinking about, and of realizing, our communities. In the end, the success of our efforts will be measured against how we have answered what we have found to be the fundamental question: how do we love all the children, of all species, for all time?

William McDonough is an architect and the founding principal of William McDonough + Partners, Architecture and Community Design

The Almere Principles explained

The Almere Principles consist of seven starting points for sustainable urban development, plus a brief introduction and conclusion. They were written especially for Almere, yet address issues which could also be at play at other places. This explanation will discuss both the local and the global dimensions of the Almere Principles.

The explanation is set up this way for each Principle. First, the text itself. This is followed by a sketch of the broader context written by William McDonough + Partners. After that, the Principle is applied specifically to the situation in Almere. This is expressed in the formulation of three major tasks for Almere.

A Dutch and English version of the Almere Principles were written simultaneously. They are equivalent to one another, yet not entirely equal. Different wording was chosen in several cases. For example, "koester diversiteit" (literally: "cherish" or "foster diversity") differs from the English "cultivate diversity". For "empower people to make the city", the well-known short form "mensen maken de stad" (literally translated, "people make the city") was chosen in the Dutch version.

The Almere Principles
For the ecologically, socially and economically sustainable future of Almere 2030

Almere, a new town designed thirty years ago on land reclaimed from the sea, will be a liveable and healthy city in 2030. It will continuously renew and transform itself, thereby strengthening the qualities of its polycentric structure and its environment. Almere will be a vital community with diverse living and working opportunities, within a beneficial abundance of open space, water, natural and cultivated landscapes that can grow and change over time.

The Almere Principles are meant to inspire and offer guidance to those involved in further designing Almere as a sustainable city in the next decades. The realization of this vision is an act of culture and the expression of an optimistic approach of the future.

1   CULTIVATE DIVERSITY
    To enrich the city we acknowledge diversity as a defining characteristic of robust ecological, social and economical systems. By appraising and stimulating diversity in all areas, we can ensure Almere will continue to grow and thrive as a city rich in variety.

*Diversity is "a precondition for processes that make life on earth possible; food, nitrogen and water cycles, the production of clean air and biomass, and the regulation of the climate system" (*4th National Environmental Policy Plan, 2001*). Diversity is as important to global health as it is to our own quality of life. In natural systems, diversity is a sign of strength; it allows ecosystems to stabilize in the face of natural catastrophe and disease, and to evolve over time. However, the benefits of diversity are not confined to natural systems. In human communities, diversity expands a culture's ability to create, innovate and thrive; it fosters a richness of engagement at all levels and strengthens community identity. Diverse economic systems are better able to weather changes in the marketplace, promote entrepreneurship, and stimulate innovation. Therefore, cultivating diversity in all realms – ecological, cultural, social, economic – strengthens health at both the local and global scale.*
WILLIAM MCDONOUGH + PARTNERS

For a new town such as Almere, expanding diversity is especially important because after thirty years it's range of diversity is still budding and shallow , compared to older, history-driven cities. Almere has an abundance of new woodland, many new residential areas, a young population with wide multicultural diversity and many new businesses. These are favourable conditions for an increasingly richer diversity in the future. But diversity must also be stimulated actively.

a   Ecological Ecologically, Almere must enlarge biodiversity, by supporting and strengthening the blue-green fabric, by differentiating management and – at regional level – by extending and improving the water and wetlands character of the Oostvaardersplassen, the Oostvaarderswold and the IJmeer/Markermeer.

b   Social Social diversity can flourish, provided there is sufficient social cohesion. This requires social structures that do justice to everyone, in which encounter and curiosity triumph over isolation and distrust. Social diversity should not only be broadened but also deepened. Compared to older cities, financial, professional and cultural elites are underrepresented, as is their contribution to the city's public life. Emerging elites should find the city an attractive place to remain. Atypical niches among newcomers deserve extra attention. The variety in residential environments and amenities should increase, particularly by emphasising private initiatives.

c   Economic To stimulate economic diversity, Almere should welcome and facilitate businesses from various sectors and sizes, making them feel at ease – from working at home to working at superregional industrial estates. Almere's economy is healthy and dynamic. Its strengths need to be developed further in ways that benefit the city as a whole. There are many opportunities, especially for sustainability-related businesses. For the sake of economic strength, Almere needs more – and higher – educational institutions.

2   CONNECT PLACE AND CONTEXT
    To connect the city we will strengthen and enhance her identity. Based on its own strength and on mutual benefit, the city will maintain active relationships with its surrounding communities at large.

All inhabitants of an ecosystem are interdependent. As global and local communities become inextricably linked, the boundaries of ecosystem have blurred; local problems have become global problems, and in the same way, local solutions have the power to change the world. Thus, every community is involved in maintaining the earth's health – economically, socially, ecologically – and we all must work together in creative ways for the success of the whole. This important work begins at home. By deeply engaging with our local communities and their social, cultural and economic forces, and by connecting to local energy and material flows, we can create sustaining economies, communities and ecologies that, in turn, positively contribute to both regional and global health.
WILLIAM MCDONOUGH + PARTNERS

Such interdependence takes concrete shape in the urban system. No city can lead an autonomous, isolated existence. That is especially true for Almere, which was designed as an integral part of the 'north wing' of the Randstad (the conurbation of Western Holland). In the future, Almere will also be inseparable from the economic, social, cultural and infrastructural networks that unite the urbanised central area of the Netherlands.

a   Identity   Almere now faces the task of clarifying its identity. If Almere is no longer an offshoot of the needs and wants existing elsewhere, what exactly is it? Commonalities can be found in the unique spatial and social characteristics of this *new town* on reclaimed land, in the original and still convincing concepts of the 'godfathers of Almere', in its special relationship with the water and the marine environment – and with the recent and age-old history of the area. This inquisitive attention for the *genius loci* and Almere's own identity should not be cast in the mould of narcissism, but as a way of creating and exhibiting cultural self-awareness. Identity is a human quality. The future identity of the city will be shaped over many years, by the commitment, efforts and actions of its inhabitants.

b   *All-sidedness*   Almere must use its unique position on the edge of the Randstad and its farmland for a more all-rounded approach. The physical, social and economic relationships with Amsterdam and Schiphol Airport will continue to be crucially important, which will be further elaborated in the "Dubbelstad" or double-city concept. Additionally, Almere should intensify its ties with the surrounding areas of the Gooi, Eemstreek, Utrecht, Zeewolde, Gelderland, Overijssel, IJmeer, West-Friesland, Lelystad and Lelystad Airport. Almere should be particularly aware of its many international connections, such as the places of origin of its multicultural population, its economic relations with Schiphol Airport or the long-distance routes of migrating birds that converge in an "aviary hub" near Almere.

c   *Connections*   Almere faces a special challenge in removing the many obstacles and snags that still affect its ecological, social, economic, physical and mental networks. In particular, the infrastructure for public transport (trains, buses, new modalities) and cars urgently needs improvement. An inaccessible city is a city with a handicap.

3   COMBINE CITY AND NATURE
    To give meaning to the city we will consciously aim to bring about unique and lasting combinations of the urban and natural fabric, and raise awareness of human interconnectedness with nature.

Humans have an innate need to connect to nature. Studies have shown that providing connections to nature increases health and productivity in office workers, improves rates of recovery and reduces pain levels among the sick, lowers stress, and raises cognitive levels. The connection between nature and humans is not merely psychological; we rely on nature's abundance for our very existence. Clean air, water and soil feed our communities and provide the building blocks, both literally and figuratively, for their growth. Even the most urban conditions still feel the heat of the sun, experience the change of the seasons, and participate in nature's cycles. Raising awareness of this interconnectedness promotes responsibility and respect for nature, and encourages new models of growth that will enhance and and sustain the natural world.
WILLIAM MCDONOUGH + PARTNERS

The urbanisation of Almere will not be done at the expense of nature, but in partnership with nature. This pursuit has a lengthy history. From the start, Almere's designers have endeavoured to see city and nature, not as opposites or enemies, but as two phenomena that could coexist at all levels, as a matter of course. At the highest level, the city has found a natural counterpart in the internationally-recognised wetlands of the Oostvaardersplassen. On a meso-level, the separate urban cores and greenbelts offer countless opportunities for natural expression. Even at the lowest level, urban development opens up avenues for natural development, which in turn raises the perceptual and economic value of the residential environment.

a   Maintain Almere's task is to nourish and conserve this unique, natural network for the future – not only because of its natural qualities, but also because of its enormous value for urban daily life. Nature's strength is that it constantly creates its own opportunities. Time will deepen the existing green structure; the city and nature will age and mature, creating a new, surprising balance between the city and nature.

b   Utilise A continuous effort is needed to utilise the opportunities afforded by nature. One should not regard nature as a patient, but as a vein of life. Spatial design should connect nature with the city at each scale level – from that of the Oostvaarderswold to that of the vegetation-covered roofs or bird-nest-friendly construction methods, from contact with nature by touring marshes to generation of wind or solar energy.

c   Combine If we treat nature and city strictly as separately sectors, we do them both injustice, as well as ourselves. But if we are alert to and look for combinations undogmatically, we can turn our efforts towards the city and nature without a sense of guilt. Nature can lift urban functions to a higher plane and, *vice versa*, so that both can flourish. It is up to Almere to ensure that this happens.

4   ANTICIPATE CHANGE
    To honour the evolution of the city we will incorporate generous flexibility and adaptability in our plans and programs, in order to facilitate unpredictable opportunities for future generations.

Just as nature constantly evolves, our understanding of the right action to take in a given situation shifts as we learn more about the world. Plans and programs are only sustainable if they can adapt over time to accommodate an unknown future. Incorporating flexibility and adaptability from the outset maximizes the value of time, materials, and energy invested while creating a valuable legacy for this and future generations.
WILLIAM MCDONOUGH + PARTNERS

From the very beginning, Almere was conceived as a framework for growth. It is a textbook example of planning for uncertainty. At the start, it was uncertain what the population of the city would be. It might be 125,000, but then again it might be twice as many, partly depending on regional and national developments. Such uncertainty did not fit the blueprint planning of the final, refined image of a city. Instead, it needed a solid, carefully considered composition of green and open space that could be used immediately, but which also left room for later interpretation and transformation. The flexibility and spatial surplus for the long term can be found throughout the city – even in the city centre, which has waited decades for the right moment to come of age. Even the wooded outline is not eternal or unchanging. Its limited forestation will give way to a richer diversity, making way for special functions, such as the Kemphaan urban estate.

a   Permanent spatial surplus Almere must continue this good habit of spatial surplus and flexibility. Now that the city is entering a new phase, the planning should be seen as an estafette to be passed on to future generations. The constant aim of this prolonged estafette is an urban community in which each generation can develop its full potential, strongly supported rather than impeded by the legacy of previous generations.

b   Changing elaboration Almere must continue this tradition of planning for uncertainty, while simultaneously changing the way it is elaborated. Until now, Almere could draw from a vast acreage of land, which was intended for urban development from the beginning, and which could be used for agricultural purposes in the interim. With the Scale Jump, the end of this acreage is in sight. It is still possible to reserve hectares of open space but, in the spirit of cradle-to-cradle, there will be an additional focus on the reversibility of urban intervention.

c   Mental surplus Almere faces the challenge of creating a 'mental surplus' in its planning methods and policies. The current, often irksome and frustrating laws, rules, standards, protocols, work procedures, legal constructions and financial conventions should ensure flexibility and space for the future. Visionary views are necessary but not enough. Developing and realizing plans that break new ground and focus on a distant time horizon should also become the obvious thing to do in daily professional practice.

5 CONTINUE TO INNOVATE
To advance the city we will encourage improved processes, technologies and infrastructures, and we will support experimentation and the exchange of knowledge.

Solutions to the challenges facing our world today will require new approaches, ones that continuously reexamine our society, our economy and our relationship to the environment. Experimentation and innovation are essential; by inventing new models that are freely shared we can build ecologies, communities and economies that transcend today's challenges and grow health and abundance for our grandchildren.
WILLIAM MCDONOUGH + PARTNERS

Almere is ideally suited for this innovative task. For thirty years, the city has been a refuge, a breeding ground and a laboratory for innovation. This pioneering spirit can be found in the city's inhabitants, its companies and in the approach taken to further development. The unremitting will to improve and innovate will exist in the future and could become even stronger.

a   Innovation and sustainability In future, Almere should link this innovative strength to its choice of sustainable urban development. Many of the sustainable interventions, processes, techniques and materials that Almere is pursuing on a grand scale still require further development for practical application. That will require a favourable climate for research, experiment and innovation, with a direct link to Almere's experience and with a national or international aura. This should attract university and other research institutes, including specialist companies. The combination of sustainability and innovation will create many magnificent opportunities. It is up to Almere to make the most of them.

b   Concentration and accumulation of knowledge
Innovation is not merely discovering something new; it is also a means of putting good, existing ideas into practice. This is another challenge that Almere faces. The city can speed up its development by collecting and utilising existing ideas on sustainability, which have often seasoned and matured for many years. Almere must ensure that theory and practice, application and evaluation are part of a continual interaction that actually encourages knowledge and expertise. In this way, Almere can become a centre of knowledge and activity in the area of sustainability. This will contribute to the city's national and international economic profile, while also benefiting indirectly from these innovations.

c   Institutional innovation The success of innovation in practice also demands mental, instrumental and managerial innovation. Innovation implies a willingness to depart from the familiar and to break new ground, without fearing unknown risks. The regulations and work procedures require constant innovations. Almere's government organisation should serve as a model.

6   DESIGN HEALTHY SYSTEMS
To sustain the city we will utilize 'cradle to cradle' solutions, recognizing the interdependence, at all scales, of ecological, social and economic health.

We can move towards having only positive impacts by using nature as a model. Cradle to cradle, a positive regenerative design approach modeled on nature, has three main principles; namely, waste equals food, rely on renewable energy sources, and respect diversity. These simple concepts can have profound effects not only on the health of our community, but that of the region and the world. Renewable energy eliminates the environmental degradation associated with conventional energy production. Recapturing technical nutrients in closed loops eliminates the need for raw material and landfills. Healthy soils, and healthy habitats, are created as the biological wastes are safely composted. These solutions not only have environmental benefits; they are opportunities for new business models, thereby stimulating the economy, and they create a better quality of life for everyone.
WILLIAM MCDONOUGH + PARTNERS

Almere realises that the Scale Jump – 60,000 additional houses between the years 2010 and 2030 – affords a unique opportunity for an effective, large-scale system innovation to sustain the city. The existing city, as well as the future urban areas, can profit from this effort. In elaborating its future, Almere draws on the inspiration of the *Hannover Principles* and the *Cradle to Cradle* philosophy of Michael Braungart and William McDonough. In these approaches, sustainability is not presented as a matter of guilt and penance, but as a positive, far-reaching design issue – 'remaking the way we make things' – with an alluring futuristic view:

'Wouldn't it be wonderful if, rather than bemoaning human industry, we had reason to champion it? (…) If new buildings imitated trees, providing shade, songbird habitat, food, energy, and clean water? If each new addition to a human community deepened ecological and cultural as well as economic wealth? If modern societies were perceived as increasing

assets and delights on a very large scale, instead of bringing the planet to the brink of disaster?' (from: *Cradle to Cradle*)

a   Mentality Almere will also view the transformation task as a design task, as a radical but realistic revision of all our work procedures. While technique serves, mentality is crucial. Urban systems should not be approached as ennobled installation techniques, but as fully-fledged, complex design tasks to enable the great leap towards sustainability. As a city below sea level, Almere should be deeply aware of the need for deliberate, intelligent efforts to bring about a drastic reduction in mankind's contribution to climate change. A stimulating climate for change suits Almere well.

b   Hardware Almere's aim is to let this mentality permeate into each area. The challenge is to implement sustainability in the *hardware* of the city, in the water management and in the public utilities for water, energy, waste and transport that serve the city, day in and day out. The aim is to bring about, wherever possible, a future with an abundance of clean, renewable energy and high-quality recycling of water, waste and raw materials. In every urban development plan, the healthiest options (walking, cycling, public transport) should always be the most obvious and attractive ones.

c   Staying on course Besides a strict, clear design, the sustainability of urban systems requires consistency, willingness and ability to proceed with the chosen design patiently over a long period. Almere has demonstrated that it can do so, based on the good design choices made in the past, such as its unique public transport system and the abundant presence of greenery. The choice for sustainability must be a sustainable choice.

7   EMPOWER PEOPLE TO MAKE THE CITY
    Acknowledging citizens to be the driving force in creating, keeping and sustaining the city, we facilitate opportunities for our citizens to pursue their unique potential, with spirit and dignity.

As stated by the United Nations Environmental Program, "an informed citizenry is the best guarantee of environmental stewardship." The sustainability movement was founded as part of the search for economic and social justice, and even the Bruntland definition of sustainability, "meeting the needs of the present without compromising the ability of future generations to meet their needs," emphasizes social concerns. A sustaining community is one where every person is empowered and engaged in shaping the future. It is only when these needs are met can we achieve true economic, ecological and environmental sustainability.
WILLIAM MCDONOUGH + PARTNERS

Almere believes that the public should have much more influence on the development of the city. People 'make' the city, spatially and socially, individually but even more so collectively. As a matter of principle, they should have the leeway to do so according to their own needs. Individual freedom, emancipation and social cohesion, self-realisation, self-organisation and self-regulation are the key words. Much more leeway is needed for public initiatives in housing and in the spatial and social life of neighbourhoods and districts. Cultivating responsibility and cohesion strengthens the community. This makes Almere appealing as an 'emancipation machine' for newcomers, along with those already living there who want to stay.

a Planning Almere should develop other types of plans for this – deliberate, powerful, based on the main outlines of the social and spatial framework, reserved yet generous within these outlines. The first concrete expressions are the large-scale programme for private housing commission ('I am building my house in Almere'), incentives for new types of 'co-commissioning', and the initiative for developing a 'socially sustainable district', Almere Hout Noord.

b Self-organisation and sustainability Self-organisation provides opportunities to embed socially the pursuit of sustainability. Ecological sustainability and the fostering of broad-based health issues could provide important, inspirational themes for social organisation. Technical ingenuity and design quality serving ecological solutions blend perfectly with a tightly-knit social dimension. The municipality should support sound bottom-up efforts that encourage civil expertise.

c Knowledge and healthcare Whether people will really 'make' the city – and make it better and more beautiful – will depend on the capabilities of its inhabitants to arrange the course of their own lives independently, well informed and without fear. In this regard, a good education and a sound healthcare system are essential conditions for *empowerment*. This should be *par excellence* at every level, so that both the old and new inhabitants of Almere will feel at home to develop their capacities in this favourable climate – and to invest enthusiastically in Almere's future.

The words of the Almere Principles will come alive and become meaningful through human action, by incorporating them on each level into every design for the city as whole.

In the old Almere style
In search of Almere principles
avant la lettre

FRED FEDDES

… introduction …

The Almere Principles are meant to serve as a guide for the sustainable urban development of Almere in the coming thirty to forty years. Anyone looking this far forward, will instinctively look just as far into the past.

Forty years ago, Almere did not even exist. "The construction of the cities along the IJmeer, across from the Gooi, will be able to start around 1975," wrote the government in the *Tweede nota over de ruimtelijke ordening in Nederland* [Second spatial planning memorandum] from 1966. As if in a time machine, we are propelled backwards by this one sentence, to a world which by now is hardly conceivable. The dikes of Zuidelijk Flevoland were not closed, the water was still there, the reclamation had yet to begin, and the cities yet to come, existed only in memoranda with long names. The bare fact that something urban would eventually arrive in the southwestern corner of the polder had already been known for a couple of years – ever since the publication of the policy documents, *De ontwikkeling van het Westen des Lands* [The development in the western part of our country] (1958), the first *Nota inzake de ruimtelijke ordening van Nederland* [Spatial planning memorandum of the Netherlands] (1960), and the *Structuurplan voor de Zuidelijke IJsselmeerpolders* [Structural plan for the Southern IJsselmeer Polders] (1961) – but that was just about all. The area did not even have a name yet.

Yet, this one sentence uttered in 1966, is, in one sense, incredibly accurate. It does not mention that a city will be built, but in fact states 'cities', in the plural. The concept of an urban development with several cores already existed at

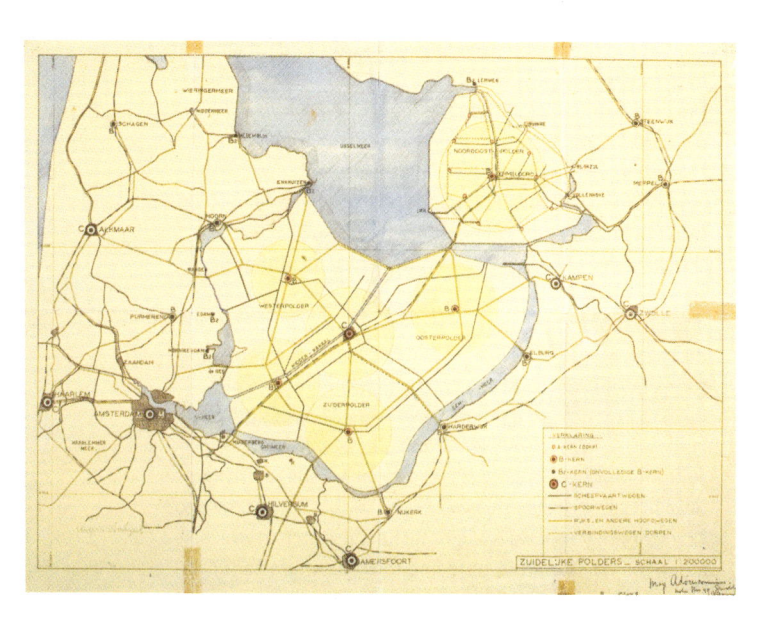

1 DIENST DER ZUIDERZEEWERKEN [AUTHORITY FOR THE ZUIDERZEE WORKS], SOUTHERN POLDER, DESIGN OUTLINE (1949)

In this design from 1949, the three future polders, Eastern and Southern Flevoland and the Markerwaard still look like introverted farmlands. The design with a central main location surrounded by several smaller cores resembles an enlarged version of the Noordoostpolder [Northeast Polder]. At this point, there was no Randstad-related urbanisation in sight.

the time, even though research into the desired urban form had not officially begun. This research commenced in 1968, the first result of which was the report, *Verkenningen omtrent de ontwikkeling van de nieuwe stad "Almere" in Flevoland* [Explorations regarding the development of the new city of 'Almere' in Flevoland] (1970). It was followed by other documents including *Almere 1985* (1974) and the *Structuurplan Almere* [The structural plan for Almere] (1983).

The question now is: at the time, was Almere invented and designed on the basis of a set of principles – points of departure, doctrines or fundamentals which link the elevated ideal to practical guidelines? What were Almere's principles at that time? Do the Almere Principles as we know them today represent a break with history, or are they actually a next step on a course that was set out upon a long time ago? The story that follows is a light historical sketch in which, along the way, we attempt to find the most important principles *avant la lettre*. Unlike the Almere Principles in their current form, they were not always laid out neatly, in a row. Some of these principles were expressed explicitly in words at the time, whereas the determinative aspect of others may only be seen after the fact. The heart of the search occurred in the period between 1966 and 1971, and ended at the official establishment of the municipality in 1984, when, although Almere was far from reaching the end of its development, its foundations had been laid. The subheadings in this document are loosely derived from the new set of Almere Principles; the reason for this is not to project them onto the past in a linear fashion, but because a surprising kindred spirit often speaks from both the old and new principles.

… the new city built on land reclaimed from the sea …
Almere marks the end of a long history of new settlements in newly reclaimed polder land. Over the course of the centuries, three primary motives may be identified for reclaiming stretches of land in the wetlands of the Netherlands: it was done for the sake of water management, for agriculture, and habitation.

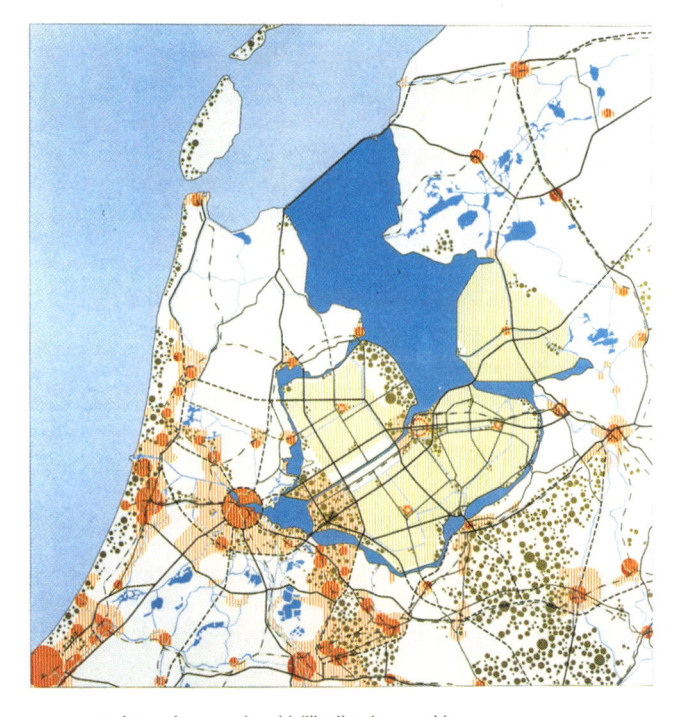

een struktuurplan voor de zuidelijke ijsselmeerpolders

2 DIENST DER ZUIDERZEEWERKEN, EEN STRUKTUURPLAN VOOR DE ZUIDELIJKE IJSSELMEERPOLDERS [A STRUCTURAL PLAN FOR THE SOUTHERN IJSSELMEER POLDERS] (1961)

For the first time, a large 'area within an urban atmosphere' in the southwestern corner of the polder is shown on the map. The city and the roads network continue on into the Markerwaard, connecting the region to Amsterdam along two sides. The dots on the map represent woodlands; in 1961, an urban entity comprising a great deal of greenery has already been anticipated.

The low-lying areas of the Netherlands somewhat resembled a Swiss cheese in the Middle Ages, the result of water eating away incautiously cultivated land. Since that time, centuries' worth of work has been put into reversing the process by reclaiming land since covered by ponds and lakes. As technical, organisational and financial capabilities increased, it became possible to do this on an increasingly larger scale. In closing off and impoldering the Zuiderzee, water management motives again played a leading role: the coastline was shortened, the inland sea was controlled, the surrounding water management was improved. Saltwater became freshwater.

In designing the polder, the water management regime became omnipresent in the form of the drainage system created by ditches, main drainage channels and canals. However, as the power of the pumping stations increased, it was possible to render the water system more broadly meshed and thereby less visible. The founders of Almere were, "with the aid of highly perfected technical resources, capable of getting rid of nearly every spatial obstruction", according to the *Structuurplan* from 1983. This does not alter the fact that the polder is an essentially unsustainable thing: water must be pumped out of it day in and day out in order to keep it dry. Its elementary existence demands a continuous supply of energy.

Nearly all of the reclaimed land became agricultural land. This was an obvious linking of interests. The reclaimers had vast acreages of rationally classified land on offer, which the ever-modernising agricultural sector needed. The room for other functions increased only gradually. One hundred percent of the Wieringermeer was a farming polder, and eighty percent of the Noordoostpolder, but in Zuidelijk Flevoland only a third was designated for this purpose.

For a long time, residential objectives were subservient to agriculture. Yet, for centuries, polders had not only offered space for farming villages, but also for suburban residential forms such as the gentrified farms and country estates in the Beemster and the Watergraafsmeer areas. This was where well-to-do city-dwellers could live close to the cities, yet still be out in the country, in a comfortable, paradisiacal

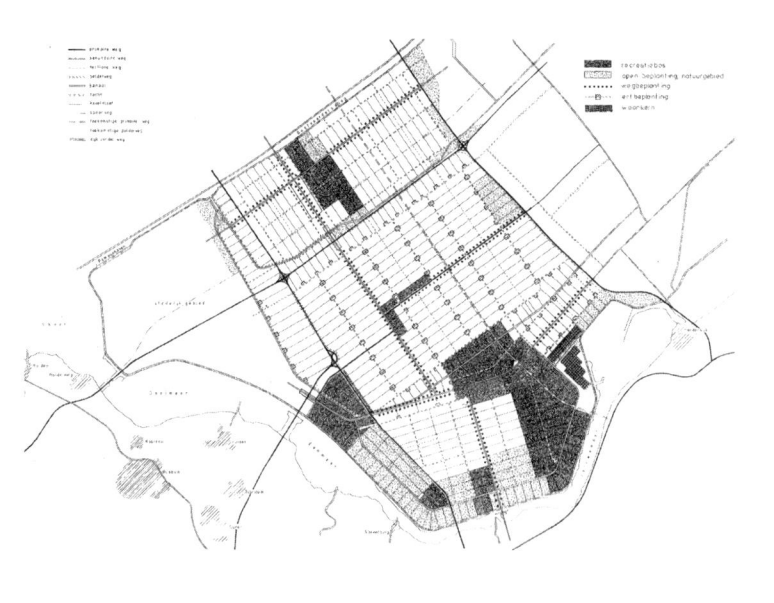

3 RIJKSDIENST VOOR DE IJSSELMEERPOLDERS [STATE AUTHORITY FOR THE IJSSELMEER POLDERS], VERKAVELINGSPLAN ZUIDELIJK FLEVOLAND [SUBDIVISION PLAN OF SOUTHERN FLEVOLAND] (1968)

As Southern Flevoland is reclaimed, the RIJP prepares for the next phase by drawing subdivision plans for farmland and forests. The tip of the polder where Almere is to be located is empty for the time being. The city will start here with a *tabula rasa*.

summer house or bower that was easily superimposed on the reclaimed land.

The new city of Almere was supposed to be a twentieth-century version of these paradisiacal residences, not destined for the elite of the Golden Age, but instead for the up-and-coming middle class of the welfare state. They were exchanging the crowded city for the polder to enjoy the luxuries of central heating and their own gardens. "For me, the whole Almere project was the realisation of an ideal", comments urban planner Teun Koolhaas in *Peetvaders van Almere* [Godfathers of Almere] (2001): "In the past, members of the aristocracy were the ones leaving the cities to build country estates. And now, thanks to our effective tax system and a high level of education, we were given the opportunity to build a country estate for a quarter of a million people."

... anticipate change ...
Even though Almere is not a farming town, its creation is closely linked to the farming polder. The city was designed in a recess in the agricultural subdivision, as is handsomely depicted in the *Verkavelingsplan Zuidelijk Flevoland* [Subdivision plan of Southern Flevoland] from 1968. Even more importantly, Almere was developed by the Rijksdienst voor de IJsselmeerpolders (RIJP) [State authority for the IJsselmeer polders], which was an old hand at creating new farmland. The two top men at the RIJP, W.M. Otto (director from 1963–1976) and R.H.A. van Duin (assistant-director from 1963–1976, director from 1976–1989), had both enjoyed an education at the Agricultural University of Wageningen and made no secret of this.

Every new city has an agrarian dimension, as Dirk Frieling mentions in *De wortels van Almere* [The roots of Almere]: "As a new city, Almere is part of the larger history of the colonisation of the world. The original significance of the word 'colonus' is farmer. Originally, a colonia was a farmstead." However, thanks to the leading role played by Otto and Van Duin, in Almere, this correlation was very direct and personal. "Of course I'm just a 'green farmer'", Otto says, describing himself coquettishly in *Peetvaders van*

Fig. XIII 6.2.

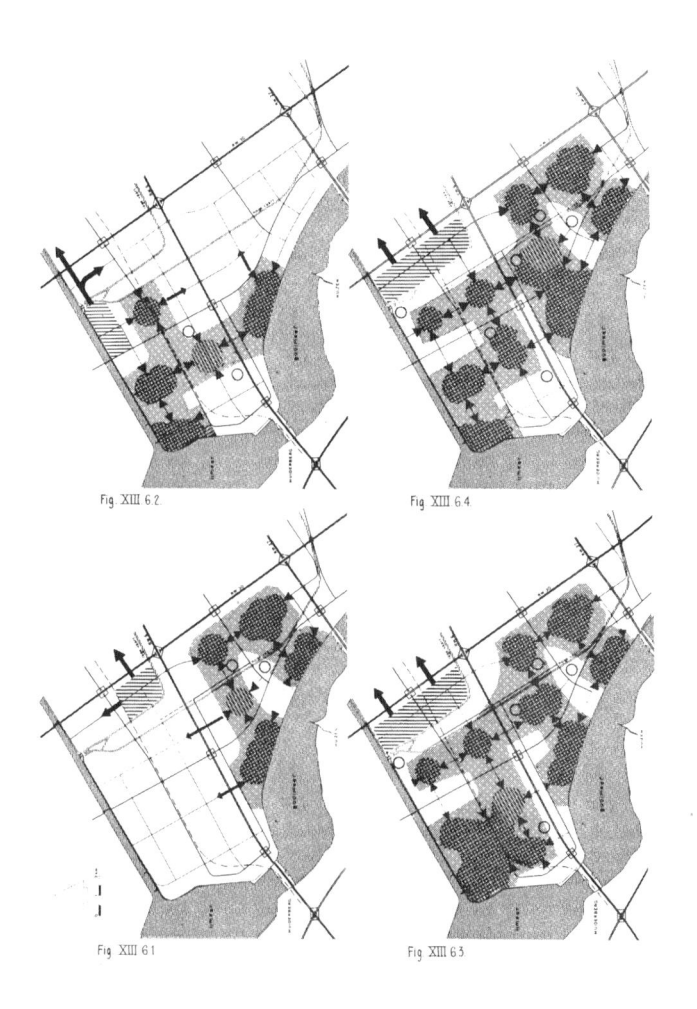

Fig. XIII 6.4.

Fig. XIII 6.1.

Fig. XIII 6.3.

4 RIJKSDIENST VOOR DE IJSSELMEERPOLDERS, VERKENNINGEN OMTRENT DE ONTWIKKELING VAN DE NIEUWE STAD "ALMERE" IN FLEVOLAND [EXPLORATIONS REGARDING THE DEVELOPMENT OF THE NEW CITY OF 'ALMERE' IN FLEVOLAND] (1970)

Almere must be a composite of several residential cores, alternating with green in a tight grid of roads, according to this proposal from 1970. It has not yet been established where the cores will be located, nor their sequence of development. These schematic maps show various possibilities. Each sphere is an 'urban concentration' with some 20,000 inhabitants.

Almere. In the same book, Van Duin said: "I ultimately view 'green' as the carrier of the urban structure. Once you get rid of this aspect, it will never return. Agriculture has always been a forerunner of urbanisation."

This is an important historical design principle for Almere. In looking back, urban planning in the hands of the RIJP resembled a special type of rational agriculture. In a manner of speaking, Almere had to become a well-balanced mixed business which incorporated good combinations of crops, a clever sequence in time, and a flexibility sufficient enough to counterbalance any surprises which have the tendency to occur in the existence of a farm or a city. The agricultural engineers rendered the enormous scope of the task more manageable by treating Almere as a region composed of a collection of fields to be worked individually within a sturdy landscape framework. They treated the huge margin built into the estimates of the future population, ranging from 125,000 to 250,000, calmly and pragmatically, much like a potato farmer who knows how unsure and variable future crop yields can be, and who gets on with his work nonetheless. "We started with round figures," said Van Duin. It was not terribly refined yet, but that didn't matter; the refinement would come later. You have to plough before you can sow. An important quality in these initial years of Almere in the late 1960s was the ability to view urban development as being a case of patient work under uncertain circumstances, as a long-term process of cultivation, growth and ripening in which immaturity is a phase rather than a problem. The city is not built, it is planted, and will grow as a landscape in which a great deal can still change.

This was not a fashionable approach at that time. Proper urban planners looked down upon the approach taken by the 'farmers', yet had few alternatives to offer in the crucial early phase. "While all of you there in Delft were arguing about who should save the world, it was people from Wageningen [university] who ended up in key positions in your field", sneered the architect Frank van Klingeren in 1976. Looking back, the Wageningen primacy was not detrimental to the design of Almere. The 'anti-urban' design from that period allowed qualities to emerge which are still

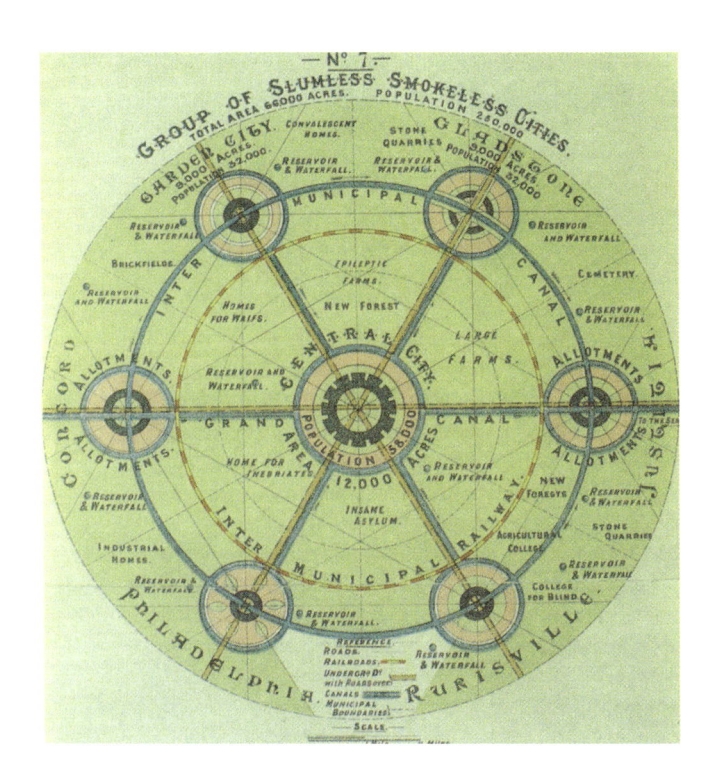

5 EBENEZER HOWARD, DIAGRAM 7, GROUP OF SLUMLESS SMOKELESS CITIES (1898)

Around the turn of the 20th century, Ebenezer Howard devised the concept of the Garden City, where town and country co-existed in a profound state of harmony. He demonstrated how seven of these garden cities could collectively form an urban landscape with 250,000 inhabitants. Due to the model's similarities to the model for Almere, this diagram was also depicted in the *Structuurplan Almere* from 1983.

highly valued, and which also have proved to be a fertile soil for further urban growth. Perhaps a bunch of 'green farmers' were needed to understand the 'organic' in 'organic urban development'.
After the contours of the settlement had thus arisen from the polder, they gradually filled themselves in with an urban character, from outside and from within.

… people make the city …
Before we discuss the continued creation of the city, it is important to realise that Almere was, for the most part, devised by a small group of people. The first maker of the city is actually the least well-known: L. Wijers, MSc., urban planner at the Dienst der Zuiderzeewerken [Authority for the Zuiderzee Works] and author of *Een structuurplan voor de Zuidelijke IJsselmeerpolders* [Structural plan for the Southern IJsselmeer Polders] from 1961. He was the first person to draft plans for an 'area within an urban atmosphere' in the southwestern corner of the new polders. It was an accurate delineation of the region for the future Almere. All of his followers remained within his lines.
The starring roles were then played by the two RIJP board members, Otto and Van Duin. Starting in 1968, Van Duin worked with a small team on the report *Verkenningen* [Explorations], and in 1971 Projektburo Almere was founded, which consisted of some twenty-five people and was led for many years by Dirk Frieling. They were the ones who plotted out the city of a quarter of a million inhabitants.
Later on, more and more people became involved in the development of the city, such as the pioneers, many of whom remained involved with the city their entire lives. Almere introduced new forms of involvement and participation, and at present, the municipality explicitly invites all citizens to get involved in the continued development of the city, under the mottos 'I'm building my home in Almere' and 'people make the city'. However, this was not the case in the beginning. Those who were most concerned about the future of Almere, namely the city's future residents, hadn't arrived yet. Many were not even aware that they would ever

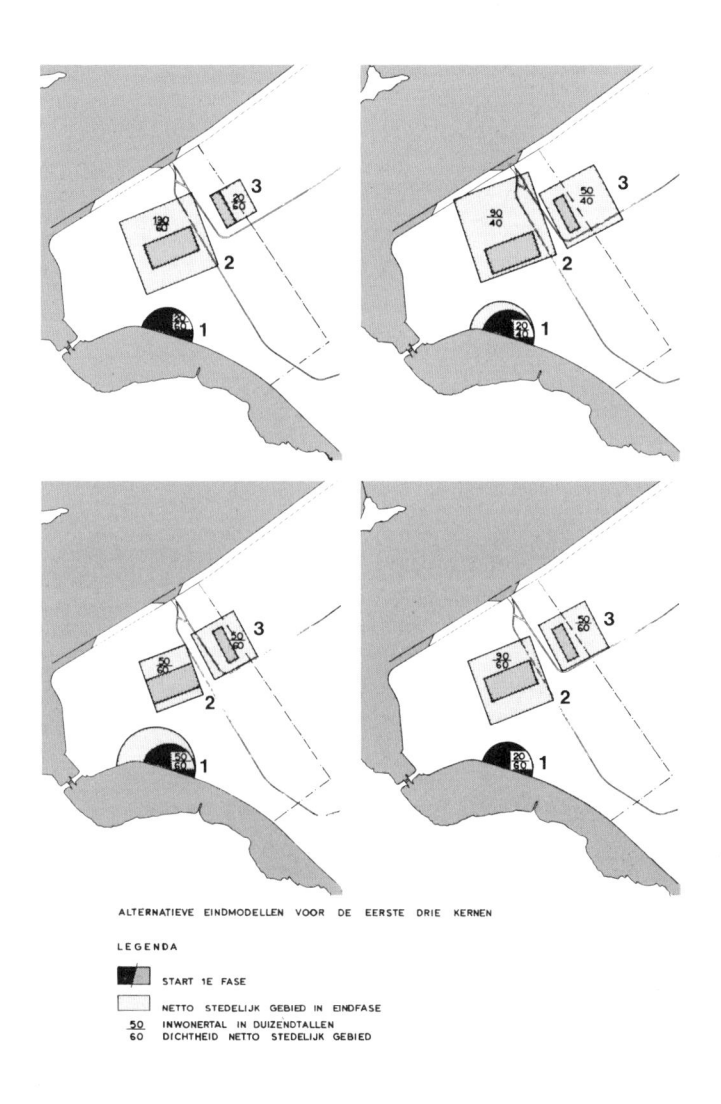

6 RIJKSDIENST VOOR DE IJSSELMEERPOLDERS, ALMERE 1985 (1974)

Working out the location and the sequence of the cores continued in the early 1970s. Choices were gradually made. The broad outlines of Almere Haven, Stad and Buiten may be identified on these maps from 1974. Their precise location and size were still being studied.

live there, let alone that they would be able to take part in decision-making processes.

According to Wil Segeren, one of the authors of the crucial report, *Verkenningen*, the fact that so few people were involved in the early phases of the development of Almere was not detrimental. "This limitation and certain level of protection was actually beneficial for the quality of Almere. I believe that it is good when a small group of people with vision concentrate on a project such as Almere. ... Of course it's great to allow everyone to have their say, but it is important to avoid always designing a city on the basis of compromises ... You cannot create beauty through reasoning, and you cannot create a vision with committees."

He made this statement in the compilation *Peetvaders van Almere*, from 2001, a collection of interviews with fourteen design pioneers. Their stories make it clear that the motto 'people make the city' applied even then, but at that time, it had a different meaning: Almere is the work of man. The foundations for Almere were laid by remarkable people who were able to bear a nearly superhuman burden, specifically that of creating a city from nothing for and on behalf of a hundred thousand other people who would later live there. Many of these people started their careers here, and the unique experience of Almere strongly helped to make them remarkable people. People make the city, and the city forms the people that make it.

Thanks to the historiography found in books such as *Peetvaders* and on websites such as *Het geheugen van Almere* [Almere's memory], the current generation of Almeerders may re-discover their city, not as a product of an anonymous machine, but as the work of driven people, who invested their intelligence, inventiveness, strength and optimism, and who were often left with a lifelong involvement as a result. This personal and long-term commitment has been one of the hidden yet essential principles of Almere, and will remain so in the future.

... connect city and context ...
Almere was not devised to be an independent city, but an addition to an already sizeable and rapidly growing urban

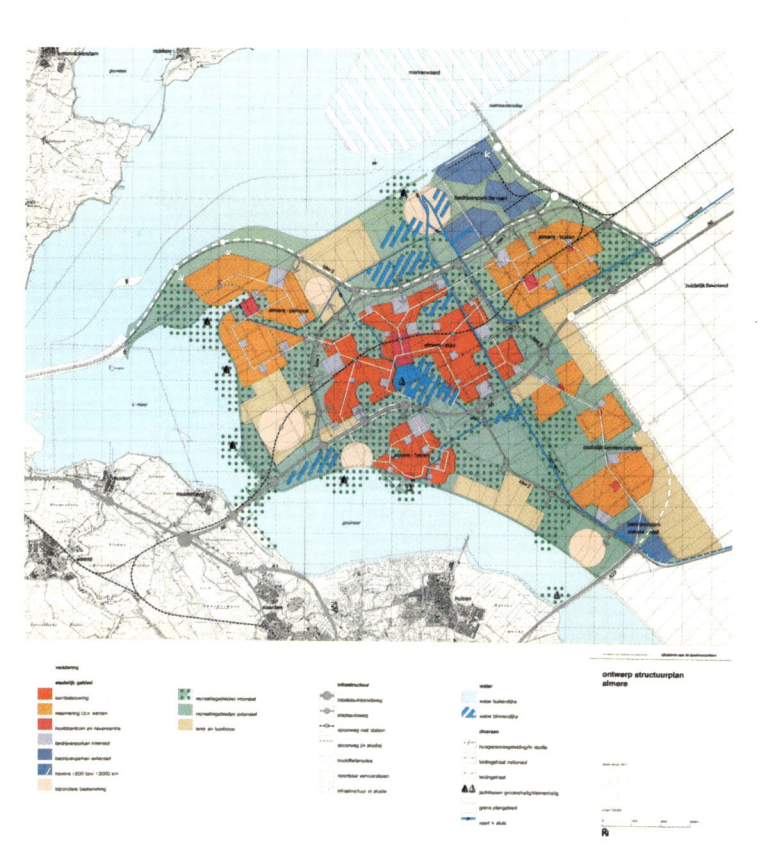

7 RIJKSDIENST VOOR DE IJSSELMEERPOLDERS, ONTWERP STRUCTUURPLAN ALMERE [STRUCTURAL DESIGN PLAN FOR ALMERE, DRAFT VERSION] (1978)

Within a couple of years, Almere changed from a chart with circles and squares to a structural design plan with recognisable spatial contours. The Weerwater appeared. A second road connection to Amsterdam ran over the Almere Pampus outside of the dike. The urgency of this connection began to increase even more once the construction of the Markerwaard became uncertain.

region. The urban context was *'het Westen des Lands'* [the western part of the country] as the area was loosely referred to in 1958. Or "the 'north wing' of the Randstad" [conurbation of Western Holland], in the words of Minister J.A. Bakker in the preface of the *Verkenningen* report from 1970. Or "the physical environment of the urban zone which extends from Alkmaar via Haarlem, Amsterdam, and other cities, the Gooi and Utrecht to Nijmegen", as is described elsewhere in *Verkenningen*.

During this period, the population of the Netherlands grew extremely rapidly, from 9.5 million in 1945 to 11.5 million in 1960 and to 13 million in 1970. Until late in the 1960s, it appeared that this speedy increase would continue, eventually exceeding 20 million by 2000. The already urbanised west was growing even faster, and the government viewed it as its solemn duty to remain one step ahead of the dangers of unliveable and overpopulated cities. An urban overspill policy was developed with plans for ten large overspill areas on the outskirts of the Randstad, one of which was Almere. In short, the connection between this city and its context was there from the very beginning, but the context was there before Almere, and the relationship was one-sided. "The table with overspill statistics … is actually the basic table for Almere," is how RIJP director Otto later summed it up. The word 'overspill' is an accurate characterisation of the foundation for Almere's existence, and this term appears no fewer than 117 times in *Verkenningen* from 1970. Almere became an alternative location for people from Amsterdam, the Gooi and Utrecht looking for homes. Socially, economically and spatially, it was scarcely connected to the rest of the Flevoland province, and it broke with the rural culture which had dominated the IJsselmeer polders up to that point.

The fact that Almere was created as a derivative of needs developing elsewhere is also evidenced in the RIJP's choice to have 90% of the residential buildings constructed as low-rise single-family homes. The arguments were the direct result of the situation in the regional residential market on the 'old' land where this type of home was underrepresented. Almere would be able to cover this deficit. As

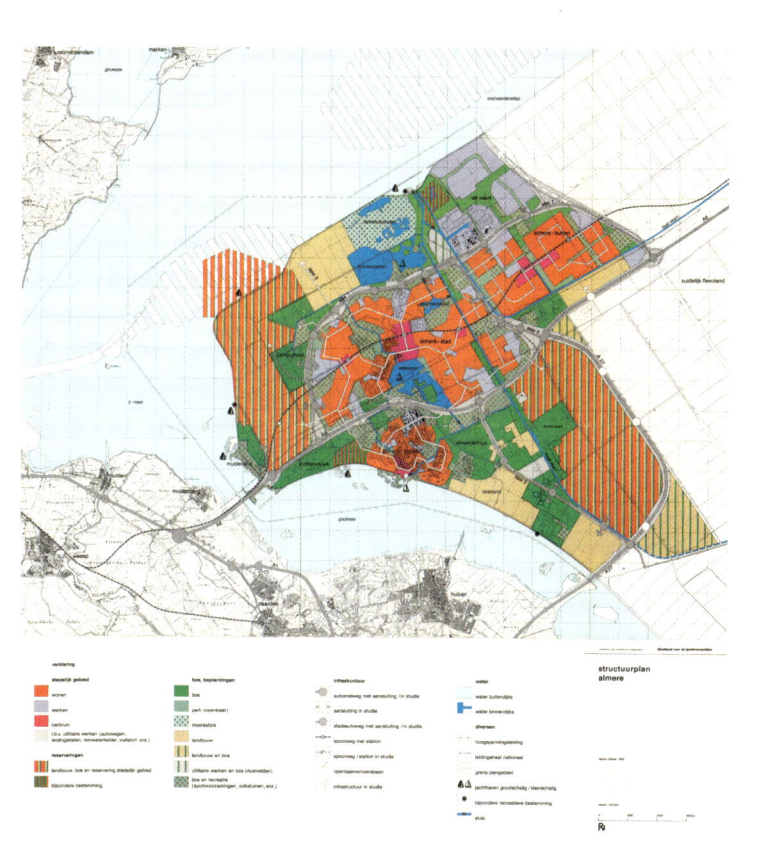

8 RIJKSDIENST VOOR DE IJSSELMEERPOLDERS, STRUCTUURPLAN ALMERE (1983)

In 1984, Almere became a municipality. This Structural Plan was thus the final chapter in the RIJP's long history of involvement with the design of the city. The future developments in the west and east are indicated in less detail than they were on the draft map from 1978. The green area between Stad and Buiten has shrunk.

described in *Verkenningen,* this was "the complementary objective Almere was supposed to fulfil with respect to the 'north wing' of the Randstad, that of initially targeting the area for suburban living". However, by contributing to the diversity in the region, a risk of monotony on a local level was developing. There was a comparable imbalance on the employment market. From the very beginning, it was clear that job opportunities were shifting to the polder less quickly and systematically than housing. On balance, Almere would still remain a commuter city for quite some time. When the idea behind Almere arose, it went without saying that after Flevoland, the Markerwaard would be the next to be impoldered. The large new polder region determined the spatial context of the cities of Lelystad and Almere, as demonstrated by the *Structuurplan* from 1961. The area would represent a new heart of the Netherlands which connected the surrounding land regions with one another. As a result of the new land, in addition to a railway, an impressive grid of motorways was designed, to "improve the entire traffic and transport network of the Netherlands", according to the government's *Tweede Nota* [Second spatial planning memorandum]. When the decision was made not to impolder the Markerwaard, this well thought-out polder composition was amputated. This had traumatic consequences for Lelystad, and the development of Almere was also handicapped as a result. The network of infrastructure that connected Almere with the Randstad suddenly appeared fairly meagre and susceptible to congestion.

In short, the relationship between Almere and the context has received a great deal of attention and care from the beginning, but it is still unstable. Long-windedness is therefore required to achieve balance.

... continue to innovate ...
The Zuiderzee project was a unique form of organised permanent education which spanned a century and a half. Seventy years of research and experimentation had already elapsed by the time the political decision for impoldering was made in 1918. The learning process continued after that, since each reclaimed polder served as a practical lesson for

9 MUNICIPALITY OF ALMERE, ONTWIKKELINGSSTRATEGIE ALMERE OOST EN WEST [DEVELOPMENT STRATEGY FOR ALMERE EAST AND WEST] (1987)

Since 1983, the formation of ideas on the development of East and West continued. The insights have changed over the course of time, but the main principles had been established early on. In East for example, sections of forest had been planted on the basis of the development strategy from 1987.

the next. The government agencies responsible for creating the polders were 'learning organisations', placing a high value on the development and retention of knowledge through scientific research and by fostering their own institutional memory. Even during the creation of Almere, the RIJP had an enormous reservoir of expertise and experience in-house; the scientific research department alone had 160 employees.

Several important lessons come together in the design of Almere. The lesson involving forestry as a design tool for example. Starting in the 1940s, the RIJP, together with the Dutch Forestry Commission and numerous outside experts (such as Dudok, Van Eesteren, Bijhouwer and Gorter), had conducted extensive studies on the use of afforestation as a structuring element in polder design. One recent result was the landscape plan for Eastern Flevoland. The knowledge acquired during this project could now be applied to the new city.

Another lesson was more painful: the lesson of Lelystad. "The urban planning 'roots' of Almere lie in Lelystad. Everything that could go wrong went wrong there", according to former RIJP director Otto. The design process involved in Lelystad had dragged for years, and had degenerated into a marathon battle between two government agencies, the RIJP and the Dienst der Zuiderzeewerken. They had a professional difference of opinion regarding the design strategy for a city with extremely uncertain population prognoses, but in addition, it was also a battle between personalities, and between two different schools of design, in short: between Delft and Wageningen. Ultimately, the design of the urban designer Cornelis van Eesteren was cast out. The Wageningers at the RIJP had won, but now had to prove that they could actually design a city.

For Almere, the RIJP wanted to start with a clean slate, with a different type of urbanisation and a different type of process. To a certain extent, the process became looser *and* tighter, more democratic *and* more hierarchical. Otto and Van Duin were at the helm. Until 1971, Van Duin worked with a small team on the outlines of the urban structure within the pattern of the *Structuurplan* from 1961. In the

Verkenningen from 1970, they studied five urban models, whereby their preference for the model with multiple cores had already become clear beforehand. "Two things were … kept out of the discussion beforehand. The choice for a city consisting primarily of low-rise buildings and the choice for a polynuclear city", Otto stated in retrospect.

In the next phase, starting in 1971, the RIJP refrained from once again engaging the services of a celebrity like Van Eesteren. Instead, the service formed Projektburo Almere, a multi-disciplinary group of ambitious young designers and scientists, the majority of whom had just graduated *cum laude*, who were given a unique opportunity right at the start of their careers, and who would identify very closely with Almere. Van Duin would later tell the tales of the 'young pups' rather cheerfully: "They did not tolerate any form of hierarchy! … They were all on a first-name basis with one another. So that meant three Henks, two Brams; it was impossible to know whom anyone was talking about". The RIJP took a risk by bringing in a self-willed new generation which could turn on the old guard, but this proved worth the risk; it was a success. The Projektburo worked as an interdisciplinary innovation machine in which chaos ostensibly reigned according to the laws of creativity, yet which nevertheless created a productive climate for the invention and trying out of new ideas. The confrontation between views which had so hindered the planning of Lelystad was now organised internally, and intensified. This occurred within a stable framework, since not only was the order of rank within the organisation established, but the sequence in time had also been determined. Almere was designed in a hierarchy of landscape above city: the landscape framework preceded the urban content and the green farmers preceded the urban planners followed on the heels of the green farmers.

Later on, Almere would provide the opportunity for numerous other innovations, for example in the areas of housing types, architecture and health care. This is not surprising in a city whose creation is so closely tied to the will to renew and to learn from the past. "I think that the relaxed and experimental attitude, the improvisational way in which

Projektburo approached a mega-project like Almere, … worked to the city's advantage", Dirk Frieling reminisces in *Peetvaders van Almere*. "The attitude of 'why not!', the insistence on giving ideas a chance still prevails!"

… combine city and nature …
The polynuclear structure of Almere – 'the urban area is comprised of several cores, located in a park-like landscape' – has already been discussed several times, and justifiably so, since this is the most determinative of Almere's spatial principles.
This principle also had its origins in the lessons of Lelystad. With Almere, the problem of the uncertain population prognoses was approached not by building one large city, but by designing several smaller cores separated by greenbelts. This design also had several other benefits. These were summarised in the 1970 *Verkenningen* as follows: the polynuclear model correlates well with the desire to construct many low-rise buildings; it allows for a great diversity in types of housing; many people will have the opportunity to live close to nature; there is variation between built-up and undeveloped areas; it offers urban planning flexibility without the drawbacks of bleak reserve areas; it results in important open spaces; it offers advantageous conditions for the 'forum function' or the possibility for public assembly; the design corresponds to the composition of the soil; it is, on balance, the least expensive alternative; and finally, there is "the need to create, to a certain degree, completed units with their own identity – also in a morphological sense – within a foreseeable period of time". It is no coincidence that this enumeration comes across as being quite convincing since the weighing of the various models against one another was rather attributed to the polynuclear model.
The origin of the multi-core model is difficult to trace with any precision. With its 'area within an urban atmosphere' which also includes 'woodlands', the 1961 *Structuurplan* appears to be ahead of its time. The emergence of the 'stadsgewest' [metropolitan district] had been discussed in professional circles for quite some time, and the concept also permeated the government's *Tweede Nota* in 1966:

"Urbanisation is no longer 'town building', but the distribution across a region of what had, up to that point, been a concentration of urban elements". When Van Duin gave his inaugural speech *Boeren, burgers en buitenlui* [Farmers, citizens and outdoorsmen] as part-time professor in Wageningen in the same year, he also discussed the concept of 'metropolitan district', but this time from a rural perspective. He envisioned a countryside of the future which would no longer exclusively be the domain of the farmer. Commuters, recreationists and nature-lovers would start to have an increasingly greater influence on the functions and the appearance of the land. A new type of region would be born out of the ingredients city, nature, recreation and agriculture, that of the metropolitan district. New types of nature areas even fit within this concept, regions which Van Duin referred to using the straight-forward engineering term of 'nature construction'. It is obvious that Van Duin had not forgotten this line of reasoning when, in the years that followed, he started working on a polynuclear Almere that did in fact resemble a metropolitan district or an urbanised region. Finally, the multi-core model may also be traced back to the RIJP's agricultural tradition. Starting in the 1920s, extensive research had been conducted into 'core patterns', in order to determine the optimum number and size of the residential cores in a new polder. A countless number of alternatives were tested for the Noordoostpolder and Eastern Flevoland. The composition of Almere appears to build on these alternatives, only incorporating cores which are larger and located much closer to one another.

After the choice had been made for a multi-core type of urbanisation, other references soon appeared as well. For example, Almere displayed similarities to the 'garden cities' which Ebenezer Howard had designed around 1900, and which had started attracting attention again around 1970. Howard devised his garden city as the solution to two equivalent problems: the increasingly impoverished country and the unhealthy city. In his vision, town and country are functionally interwoven with one another, however they are characterised by strictly separate land regimes and stringent zoning, made possible by the lack of private land ownership.

The spatial image is surprisingly subtle: the greenery penetrates deep into the heart of the city, and there are countless urban functions spread throughout the surrounding countryside. These include not only farms, nurseries, forests, allotment gardens and drinking water reservoirs which supply directly to the city, but also convalescent and care homes for orphans, the blind and deaf, alcoholics and epileptics. The green areas are not empty, but chock full. Howard had had a great deal of influence due to his social conscience and his radical ideas on land policy and new town and country relationships, yet perhaps even more intriguing was the hypnotic power and beauty of the didactic illustrations with which he expanded upon his theories. Images such as 'Diagram 7', in which seven perfectly-round garden cities together formed a 'Group of Slumless Smokeless Cities' with a total population of 250,000, appealed to people's imaginations. This diagram was also depicted in the *Structuurplan Almere* from 1983.

The creators of Almere also made references closer to home, to the Gooi [the region mirroring Almere on the 'old land']. In *Peetvaders van Almere*, Wil Segeren, one of the men involved from the very beginning, recounts how this came about: "I arrived ... at the curious discovery that the Gooi spanned an area of 14,000 hectares, just like Almere. And also had five cores, just like Almere. And that the largest core had 100,000 inhabitants, the same number we had set for Almere Stad." It was clear that Almere should not aim to compete with Amsterdam or Haarlem in terms of its urban character, but should instead emulate older suburban areas such as the Gooi.

The design of Almere was the object of a great deal of criticism in professional circles in the 1970s. The plan was supposedly 'anti-urban', and the RIJP was accused of listening too closely to 'what the people want'. Almere marked the 'commercialisation' of urban planning, and the play on words, 'Los Almeros', made its debut rather quickly. Almere had violated the fundamental rule of urban and rural planning from that time which prescribed a strict separation between 'red' and 'green'. In retrospect, it is clear that the creators of Almere were on a track that would only gradually gain appreciation, namely the path to a new, more diffuse relationship between town and country. In all of these references – Van Duin, Howard, the polder cores, the Gooi – the attention is focused just as sharply on the green as the red. The design of Almere implied the promise of a new interaction between town and country. 'Multi-core' was actually a rather unfortunate word choice since this placed the primary attention on the red of the cores, whereas the crux of this design was actually the equality of green and red. Much later the looser relationship between town and country would once again be studied in works such as *Visie Stadslandschappen* [Urban landscapes vision] (1995) from the Ministry of LNV [Agriculture, Land Management and Fisheries], and the VROM Advisory Council's recommendation *Buiten Bouwen* [Building in the countryside] (2004). Viewed from a Dutch context, these works served primarily as therapy to massage the stiff red-green relationship. After all, it was hardly a resounding success. What the one referred to as a relaxed relationship between red and green, the other viewed as making a mess of the landscape.

The promise was also only partially redeemed in Almere. The RIJP wanted to incorporate the multi-core approach consistently by forming a separate design team for each core, and also by establishing a separate municipality for each core. However, in 1984, Almere became a single municipality and inadvertently, the cores have gravitated towards one another, both in terms of programmes and spatially. Red and green turned out to be less equal than intended. Slowly, green areas which should have stayed green have been built upon, for example, between Stad and Buiten. The fact that the *Structuurvisie voor de Buitenruimte van Almere* [Structural vision for the Almere landscape] from 1978 was never officially put into practise has always remained a handicap in the integral treatment of the green areas. A single glance at the map or at the core statistics demonstrate that the comparison between Almere and Howard's garden cities is flattering: in Howard's design, 250,000 people have access to 27,000 hectares of town and country, whereas in the plans for Almere, the same number of people live on an area that is only half as large. Howard's ideal is utopian in the crucial and uncompromising role he ascribed to land ownership alone.

However, some of these missed opportunities in terms of developments are still possible. As early as 1983, in the *Structuurplan* from that same year, the case was made that 'this city was perfect' for experimenting with environmentally-friendly agriculture linked to education. Over the years, the monocultural timber forest has taken on a greater biodiversity, and red functions have started appearing here and there among the green – although these have not been asylums but more luxurious locations such as De Kemphaan urban estate.

The critics who viewed Almere as being 'anti-urban' passed judgement too soon. The design of Almere was more pre-urban than anti-urban. The RIJP 'farmers' did not build a complete city as a unified whole, but planted a relatively modest settlement over a large area which would be able to continue to grow over time, and which would perhaps eventually become a city, or not. They created the conditions for a settlement with an open future. Or, as had already provided for in *Verkenningen*, it "seems desirable to assume more or less independent concentrated clusters in the development of Almere, yet while also keeping the option open to develop a more complex urban fabric".

… design healthy systems …

The fate of many of the principles of Almere had already been sealed in 1971, when the Dutch government accepted the *Verkenningen* report as the foundation for the formation of plans and when Projektburo had been founded. The real work started after that. While construction had already begun on the individual cores (Haven in 1975, Stad in 1979, Buiten in 1983), work started on a cohesive and attractive urban system according to planning documents such as *Almere 1985* (1974), the *Ontwerp Struktuurplan Almere* [Structural design plan for Almere, Draft version] (1977) and the final *Structuurplan Almere* (1983).

Projektburo thought long and hard about the number, the size and the placement of the housing nuclei in relation to one another, the transport system, the role of water both inside and outside of the city, the route for the A6 and the railway, the recreational use of the greenbelts, and about technical systems such as district heating. Many of these choices were already present in rudimentary form in *Verkenningen*, for example that for public transport, "one possibility is a fully or partially free lane in order to prevent unnecessary congestion". However, the task now at hand was to give these ideas concrete shape, turning them into actual urban forms and systems. The city went from being a diagram to a region. Care was taken in the design with respect to the perception of the spaces, the lines of sight, and a great number of social aspects. During the process, some of the good intentions were cast out, while other great ideas were born. One example is the creation of a central lake, the Weerwater. For the old-school members of the RIJP, it was an almost unnatural proposal since, in their minds, they had just finished driving the water *out* of the polder, however Teun Koolhaas was able to convince them. The development of the system for public transport with its free bus lanes was also a success.

Anyone reading the plans from that time today will notice how much of the focus was on recreation. Almere was invented during the heyday of recreational policy, the era marked by the R in the name of the Ministry of CRM [Culture, Recreation and Social Work]. Leisure time and recreation represented a political-ideological issue, in which themes such as emancipation, personal development, health, welfare, social gatherings and social cohesion came together and had a major influence on spatial planning activities. Almere was designed on the basis of this vision, and the ideas involving the landscape in particular were coloured by these concepts. Not much later, the topic of leisure time withered within the grand scheme of government policy; from now on, this aspect would be determined by the logic of the marketplace. The development of Almere bears the marks of these developments. The importance of recreational space as 'merit good', as a crucial element in a healthy urban system is still recognised, yet a cohesive social-spatial concept is lacking. It is almost as if a promising system-in-the-making drifted off course halfway to its destination, and crumbled.

… cultivate diversity …
When Almere was getting its start, the circumstances for social and economic diversity were not favourable. *Verkenningen* cites several reasons for this, such as "the widespread uniform post-war urban expansion, and the fairly short period the city was given for its completion". The creators of Almere did not make it any easier on themselves with their housing decision of 90% single-family homes.

And then there was the expected one-sidedness of the criteria 'by income group'. The overspill from the old cities to Almere was, for the most part, to consist of people from the lower income groups. There is still considerable variation within these groups, and Almere strongly encouraged this diversity, for example under the motto: "Come to Almere, and bring your mother with you". One of the results of this was that Almere is now the second most multi-cultural city in the Netherlands. In spite of this, from a socio-economic viewpoint, the diversity has remained 'shallow'; the financial, administrative and cultural elite are underrepresented. This had been expected at the time, albeit in guarded terms. It was clearly a sensitive subject that had to be cautiously worded.

The problem was that diversity also tends to stand for inequality. Maintaining social inequality was not popular at the time, yet nonetheless, the creators of Almere had to accept inequality as a given, claimed the authors of *Verkenningen*. They did not use their own words to state this, but those of quoted, established experts. Such as the urban planner Willem Steigenga: "In developing plans, with respect to ideological points of departure involving a certain degree of uniformity of our society, one must adopt a position based on the reality that we live in a pluriform society which means that different systems of standards and values simply occur alongside one another". And the socio-geographer Gerard Hoekveld, who, in studying the historical growth of the urban area between Velzen and the Gooi, discovered how important exurbs are to the quality of urbanisation. The residential areas populated by the intellectuals and administrators may "act as a ... carthorse in the development of areas which were, up to that point, not important", and are, in this respect, similar to large companies or institutions such as a university.

However, the carthorse must be willing. "The point now, of course, is whether or not a physical environment can be created in Almere that is attractive enough to exert a sufficiently strong pull on the aforementioned category", according to *Verkenningen*. "It may be said in summary that, on the basis of the need for housing alone, the accent will be placed on the lower income groups, yet that in order to create an 'attractive environment', special attention will have to be placed on the construction of a 'relative excess' of more expensive homes". In short, a complete city also needs an elite and in order to lure this elite, additional efforts are required.

Against this background, it is understandable why, in 1979, Van Duin proposed building a golf course in Almere, even though there were only 4000 people living there at the time, and even though they had very little desire to play golf. By investing in a luxury facility, Almere would be able to show from the very start that it was not just a dormitory suburb, but would become a complete city where the elite were also welcome. Han Lammers, the local administrator who had been appointed in the meantime, had a different view. He rejected the plan. In doing so, he confirmed the fear expressed in *Verkenningen* that the 'ideology of equality' stood in the way of the vision of a complete city. Other disappointments included the fact that the arrival of part of the University of Amsterdam, something which had been seriously discussed in the 1970s, ended up falling through, and that Almere was unable to convince any major, specific industries to commit to the region. The examples illustrate that diversity is not something that can be forced, and that it is not free from value judgements. The forms of diversity that are valued depend on the social and political views and trends.

However, apart from that, the development of diversity has its own dynamic. The diversity of Almere continues to grow as the city gets older, and it is already considerably broader than it was in the beginning. Apart from the composition of the population, this also applies to the biodiversity and the economic activity. The *Structuurplan* from 1983 had already anticipated this. For example, with respect to ecology: "As the diversity in the landscape grows, the number of species with a chance of survival in this environment also increases". And on the economy: "As development progresses, an increasingly large range of activities will also occur within the agricultural field". The social and cultural diversity will also grow with each generation. The city is patient.

… *words come to life* …
One may deduce several historical fundamentals of Almere from the above. Almere has taken a new step in a long tradition of newly developed polder occupation. Almere has arisen from the landscape, even though that landscape had to be created simultaneously. Almere is the work of people, the work of driven individuals with a high level of personal involvement. Almere is a product of the will to learn continuously and to innovate. Almere started as a derivative of the metropolitan context and has gradually acquired its own identity. Almere was designed as a polynuclear region, with the promise of a pleasant living environment in the vicinity of urban and natural forelands. Almere was a life-size laboratory in which numerous new systems have been developed and applied in the service of a healthy environment. In an ecological, social and economic sense, Almere was rather one-sided in the beginning, yet is now on its way to developing an increasingly richer diversity.
This sounds familiar. Many of the themes which are now being discussed in the Almere Principles may be found here, in letter or spirit. A major difference with the Almere Principles is the extent of their public nature. The Almere Principles have been presented, published and intended to live a public life. This was hardly the case in the past. Points of departure and objectives were neatly summed up in a memorandum or a report, as administrative and official

reminders, yet were otherwise not placed in the spotlights. Perhaps it is the Calvinistic or pragmatic streak which causes the Dutch to shy away from using big words. We do not avoid the big words entirely, but instead use them in moderation, use them fleetingly so that we can quickly proceed with the order of the day, and we prefer not to use them too often in public, since we do not wish to be accused of blowing our own trumpets.

This is why any explicit formulation of the Almere Principles *avant la lettre* is rare. The best exception to this however are the objectives from the 1974 report, *Almere 1985*, which were later reiterated in the 1983 *Structuurplan*:

1 *Almere must make a direct contribution to the resolution of today's regional problems.*
2 *Almere must keep options open for tomorrow.*
3 *Almere must offer room to everyone.*
4 *Almere must encourage the individual development of those who live there.*
5 *Almere must make a contribution to the creation and preservation of a healthy natural environment.*
6 *Almere must make a contribution to the preservation and continued development of an urban culture.*

It is an elegant and well-thought-out package of objectives. They are linked to one another in pairs: numbers 1 and 2 focus on the short- and long-term, numbers 3 and 4 on society and the individual, numbers 5 and 6 on nature and culture. They may be linked to the Almere Principles with a surprising ease. For example, "keep options open for tomorrow" dating from 1974 is related to "anticipate change" from 2008, whereas "offer room to everyone" is in the same spirit as "cultivate diversity". The elaboration on the diversity objective theme from 1974 is also recognisable: "a complete community in which all age groups, income groups, professional categories and lifestyles are represented from the very start; a collection of majorities and minorities".

The Almere Principles from 2008 may be new, but they have long and complex roots in the past. They are related to the motives, mainsprings, goals, ambitions and dreams which drove the development of Almere at the time. They are building on qualities which have already been achieved in

Almere, but also on the original promises of Almere which have, up to the present, gone partially or completely unfulfilled. They offer points of departure for placing deviations and dilemmas in perspective, and, if possible, to correct them. The Almere Principles shed a new light on the future, but just as much on the past. On the road to the future, the best values from the past come to life once again.

Fred Feddes is a journalist and writer

LITERATURE CONSULTED

JaapJan Berg et.al. (ed.), *Adolescent Almere. Hoe een stad wordt gemaakt*, Rotterdam, 2007
R.H.A. van Duin and G. de Kaste, *Het Zuiderzeeprojekt in zakformaat*, Lelystad, 1995(4)
Fred Feddes et.al. (ed.), *Oorden van onthouding. Nieuwe natuur in verstedelijkend Nederland*, Rotterdam, 1998
Dirk Frieling, *De wortels van Almere. Vier verhalen. Hazelnootlezing, 7 april 2006*, Almere, 2006
Adriaan Geuze and Fred Feddes, *Polders! Gedicht Nederland*, Rotterdam, 2005
Zef Hemel, *Het landschap van de IJsselmeerpolders. Planning, inrichting en vormgeving*, Rotterdam, 1994
Gerrit van Hezel and Aaldert Pol, *De Flevolandse geschiedenis in meer dan 100 verhalen*, Amsterdam, 2005
Gé Huismans et.al. (ed.), *Plannenatlas Almere. Chronologie van 30 jaar plannen in Almere*, Almere, 2008
Rijksdienst voor de IJsselmeerpolders, *Verkenningen omtrent de ontwikkeling van de nieuwe stad "Almere" in Flevoland*, Flevo-berichten No. 78, Lelystad, 1970
Rijksdienst voor de IJsselmeerpolders, *Almere 1985* (1974)
Rijksdienst voor de IJsselmeerpolders, *Structuurplan Almere*, Flevobericht nr. 243, Lelystad, 1983
Brans Stassen, JaapJan Berg, *Peetvaders van Almere. Interviews met bestuurders en ontwerpers*, Almere, 2001
Coen van der Wal, *In praise of common sense. Planning the ordinary. A physical planning history of the new towns in the IJsselmeerpolders*, Rotterdam, 1997

Many thanks to Dirk Frieling for his remarks on a previous version of this chapter.

The first exercise for the Principles in Almere
An impression of the introduction in April 2008

FRED FEDDES

The perspective
In his introduction to the Almere Principles on the 8th and 9th of April, William McDonough began with a reference to Thomas Jefferson, one of the most famous Americans of all time. Among other things, he was the author of the *Declaration of Independence*, the third U.S. President, a gentleman-farmer, intellectual, inventor and architect.
Jefferson's last design was his own tombstone. He limited the inscription to three things he had designed: the declaration of independence, an act for establishing religious freedom, and a university. "He did not list any of his activities, not even that he had been the President of the United States. His legacy was the only thing that mattered", according to McDonough.
With this story, McDonough was casting a glance far into the future. Even when Almere's Scale Jump has yet to begin, and the Almere Principles must still prove their worth, he asked the question: Esteemed Citizens of Almere, what will your legacy be? In doing so, he placed the Almere Principles within a long-term perspective. It was an invitation to make great gestures, to look to the horizon, to brainstorm and to work on the future of Almere, and to do all this on the basis of these principles. "Become a part of the community that is creating the legacy of the future".
What followed was an initial introduction between the Almere Principles and an engaged audience, and a first taste of the applications. This occurred in the company of three groups: members of the municipal council, Dutch experts, and stakeholders involved socially and economically in the growth of Almere. In addition to McDonough, the Minister

of VROM [Housing, Spatial Planning and the Environment], Jacqueline Cramer, was also in attendance in the main reception room of the Almere city hall. It was a special and yet unpretentious moment. As the text itself indicates: "The words of the Almere Principles will come alive and become meaningful through human action, by incorporating them on each level into every design for the city as whole". This implies that without motivated people, the Principles will remain a dead letter. And because action has only just started, the tone during these days was set by expectant optimism but also by modesty.

"I come here very humbly to be part of your story", McDonough said. At the end, Alderman Adri Duivesteijn stated: "We have been practising".

The conquest
The invitation to brainstorm was generally accepted. After two days, it appeared that the Almere Principles' existence was already self-evident. No one doubted the Principles' right to exist, none of the Principles had been declared redundant, and no major gaps had been detected. The suggestions for additions, such as more attention for the achievements of Almere's past and an increased emphasis on social aspects did not lead to a review of the Principles; a different clarification and other accents in the details were deemed sufficient. The tenor was positive. Those in attendance were eager to brainstorm on the Almere Principles, in order to arrive at a sustainable future for Almere. One of them even said: "My goal is that people should want to live in this city *because* of the Principles".

It was interesting to experience how the participants became familiar with the Principles. The Almere Principles are a highly compact document, they touch on a multitude of topics, they are profound, and they are far-reaching in their consequences. It is not a matter of course that everyone can comprehend them all at once; it is obvious that the conquest is a gradual process. And this is exactly what happened. Each discussion group started with the question about a ranking among the Principles, such as: What is the most important principle, which of the seven contains the key to the other six, which one appeals to you the most, or: where does your heart lie? This was how the Principles were unravelled, brought closer, made manageable and given a personal tone. They no longer formed a solid block, but became an active series which could be ranked according to personal insight. Anyone can tell their own story on the basis of the Principles, based on their own interests and their own involvement.

The specific stories and lines of reasoning were not discussed exhaustively during this initial introduction, yet initiatives were taken which provided an indication of how one may use the Almere Principles. The most elaborate of these was that of Dirk Frieling in his memo *How citizens can make their city* which he wrote some days later. He uses the principle 'people make the city' as his point of departure, and on this basis, reasons what can or must happen in regard to the other principles. In short: Frieling's guide starts with number 7 and plots out a course along numbers 2, 6, 1, 3, 4 and 5.

Most of those present limited themselves to determining their initial preferences. Every principle had its own group of followers, in which some made a distinction between principles which had the most personal appeal for them, and principles which were most closely associated with their work. Patterns quickly emerged in these preferences. 'People make the city' was cited most frequently as being the key principle. Among the council members, 'anticipate change' was the runner-up, whereas the experts chose 'continue to innovate' as their second preference. It is tempting to attribute this difference to both groups' work environments: politicians are there to look ahead, experts deal with innovation on a daily basis in their work. And shouldn't the emphasis on 'people make the city' be closely connected to the current social climate, in which people are feverishly looking for new alliances between public officials and citizens, and between experts and laypersons?

Confrontations
These initial choices were followed by a search for connections and contrasts. How are the Principles related to the

existing city, to the social reality, to one another? Where can conflicts occur, and what can we learn from this?

The Almere Principles are familiar concepts to many of the participants. "A great deal of what they describe dovetails with what we are already doing, such as the organisation of health care, the underground waste disposal system and the waste separation system, the plan for the 'sun island', and the fact that Almere is populated by many enterprising citizens and start-up businesses". Also, in spatial terms, Almere can use the Principles to build on existing qualities. "Take advantage of the power of the original urban design". The Scale Jump demands precision in the relationship between old and new. "As the city grows, what will happen to the existing city?"

The combination of several Principles proved to be a fruitful basis for discussion. In these confrontations, the primacy of the citizen in principle 7, 'people make the city', was frequently unleashed on the other principles, such as number 1, 'cultivate diversity', and number 4, 'anticipate change'. "How much diversity does Almere want?", some of the participants asked themselves. Diversity means vitality and surprise in a 'stimulant-rich environment', and this can be an 'impulse for tolerance', but it can also scare people off. "Many people need the security and familiarity of a daily life, with a home, children, a garden and a car. How does this relate to diversity and continual change?" One danger of diversity is "that you can end up at odds with one another". For the city, it is good to be flexible and able to anticipate, but not all citizens are eager for change in their own living environment, and with a 'NIMBY attitude' (Not In My Back Yard), they can 'lock' the city. In other words: "It is difficult to satisfy the other six principles if you can't get people on your side. This is the condition for success needed to accomplish the rest".

Then, the Principles also proved useful as a guiding principle in searching for solutions. "Cultivate diversity, but make sure a connection is still there", was one comment made, and this linked the argument for diversity to principle 2, 'connect city and context'. "Make sure that you can live together in harmony and have enough tools to overcome squabbles". In addition, it is wise to evenly dose the desire for diversity and to make distinctions at different scale levels: "Do not 'mix to the max'. At the lower scale levels, neighbourhood and district, a high degree of diversity can lead to tensions, whereas diversity at the higher scale level of the city or region as a whole is meaningful". The resistance to change can take on a positive significance by radicalising the 'people make the city' principle: "The NIMBY effect will increase as property and the influence on the process of spatial planning decrease. So give some thought to the influence the residents have on their own neighbourhood. It is not only the property or the land that's important, but also the 'ownership' of the planning process and the financial resources that counts". And: "It is a good idea to give citizen initiatives a bit of free rein. Even if the planning results are not optimal from the government's point of view, it will create a sense of solidarity in the neighbourhood". There were also questions raised regarding the combination of 'people make the city' with principle 3, 'combine city and nature': "Is sustainability a mainstream concept?" A connection was also made between Principles 5 and 6 regarding innovation and healthy systems and 'people make the city'. For example, in the story of the energy company which encourages people to be environmentally and cost-conscious in their consumption of heat, only to turn around and reap the profits themselves: that is not empowerment. Criticism was heard here and there that the Principles place too much emphasis on the spatial aspects and too little on the social dimension. "This is about people who live together; it is not the physical environment which makes the city, but the solidarity and pride". Suggestions were made to reinforce the social dimension: "Apply the sustainability principle to people. Strive to make the new city sustainably social. Eliminate the circumstances and reasons for the excess frequency of moving. Create a new neighbourhood that people will come to love, by bringing a lot of work to the neighbourhood, by offering plenty of options for children. For example, design a neighbourhood where you can walk your children to and from school".

It was interesting to notice that some topics were hardly discussed at all. Only a handful of people noticed that there is no mention of safety in the Principles, even though this used to be an unavoidable topic of political discussion not so long ago. Is there is no longer any interest in the safety theme? Or has it been incorporated into the Principles, for example in a combination of diversity, connection, empowerment and the concept of healthy urban systems? And so, the Principles churned up numerous questions and answers, doubts and suggestions. The Almere Principles seem to make it possible to ask existing questions in a new way, and within a new framework, with a view to providing a new way of answering them. They do not gloss over political differences in insight, but represent a shared vocabulary: "They transcend politics, offer a collective point of departure". This encouraged the participants to go a step further: "In addition to the seven Almere Principles, can't we also put seven Almere dilemmas down on paper?"

A movement
While the utility of the Almere Principles was being tested, a rush of ideas elaborating on this theme was released which will undoubtedly find their way to realisation in the near future. A random selection: cherish the young people who grow up here, because they are the ones who bring diversity; make Almere hip, sexy and beautiful; don't place the squares in the new construction areas on the edge of the neighbourhood, but instead right in the middle; consult *The Great Neighborhood Book*; stimulate nature at every level, up to the most urban, so that you can 'harvest fruit from the façades'; allow Almere to grow to become a Silicon Valley for sustainable business; allocate existing business premises with their affordable rent to new, creative businesses; create flexible zoning plans; change the 'energy performance label' into an 'ecological performance label'; make the most of the water; work on urban growth, but also make allowances for stagnation and shrinkage; work towards a future 'Almere Cultural Capital 2018'; and, change the slogan from 'It's possible in Almere' to 'It works in Almere'. And so forth.

It was time to get started. At the municipality, the Principles must be incorporated into the plans for the Scale Jump, but also into the council discussions and the internal organisation. One important formal step in this direction is the motion, passed on 26 June, in which the entire Municipal Council endorsed the Almere Principles as "the primary, guiding principles in the development of the entire city". The stakeholders are confronted with the same essential questions on the significance of the Almere Principles for their thoughts and actions. The Almere Principles must become an automatic point of reference in the dialogue between citizens and the council. This requires the explanation, enlistment, motivation, internalisation, and translation of the Principles for various groups into their own language, and of course, convincing results: "Create success in order to develop a support base". A platform must be created for initiatives from citizens, businesses and social institutions, which focuses on designing plans for the distant future, but also on activities which are immediately applicable for the Almere of today. In the words of one of the participants, "The Principles must serve as continual reminders for us". "This is the start of a movement", said another. The introduction was over, the future of the Almere Principles had begun.

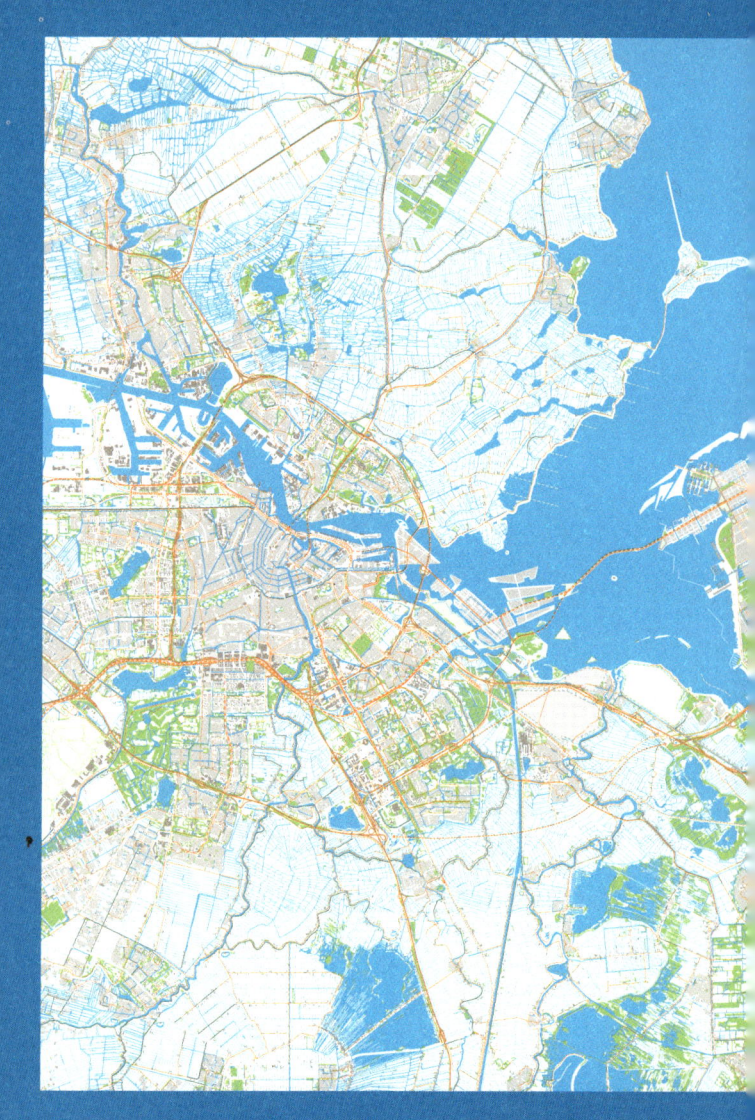

10 MUNICIPALITY OF ALMERE (ELLEN MARCUSSE) AND TEUN KOOLHAAS, ATELIER IJMEER (2006)